Stop-Motion Filming and Performance

Stop-Motion Filming and Performance

A Guide to Cameras, Lighting and Dramatic Techniques

TOM BRIERTON

AUTHOR OF

Stop-Motion Armature Machining:
A Construction Manual (2002)

Stop-Motion Puppet Sculpting:
A Manual of Foam Injection, Build-Up,
and Finishing Techniques (2004)

McFarland & Company, Inc., Publishers
Jefferson, North Carolina, and London

LIBRARY OF CONGRESS CATALOGUING-IN-PUBLICATION DATA

Brierton, Tom, 1957–
    Stop-motion filming and performance : a guide to cameras,
lighting and dramatic techniques / Tom Brierton.
        p.   cm.
    Includes bibliographical references and index.

    ISBN 0-7864-2417-6 (softcover : 60# alkaline paper)

    1. Animation (Cinematography)   2. Motion picture cameras.
3. Cinematography — Lighting.   I. Title.
TR897.5.B7522   2006
778.5'347 — dc22   2005032535

British Library cataloguing data are available

On the cover: Grim Reaper puppet by George Higham from the 2001
short *Annabel Lee* (www.poepuppet.com)

Manufactured in the United States of America

*McFarland & Company, Inc., Publishers
  Box 611, Jefferson, North Carolina 28640
    www.mcfarlandpub.com*

This book is dedicated to my parents:

Portia Brierton, for her support and encouragement
to my work in film and animation in my early years,
and for her continued support as I go on making films.

And to the memory of my late father, John (Jack) Brierton
(1931–2001), for sharing his gift of music, which I found (much later in life)
priceless and beyond any material inheritance.

Acknowledgments

I am indebted to Lance O. Soltys for sharing his knowledge in lighting and camerawork as I prepared this text. Thanks also to James Aupperle for sharing information and opinions based on his many years of work in visual effects cinematography and animation for feature films, and for his advice on the lighting chapter of this manual. Thank you, gentlemen.

Table of Contents

Preface

Stop-Motion Filming and Performance: A Guide to Cameras, Lighting, and Dramatic Techniques is a follow-up to two earlier books on stop-motion animation. The previous two — *Stop-Motion Armature Machining* and *Stop-Motion Puppet Sculpting* — were written with a more technical sensibility. This manual, while technical to some extent in its explanation of lights, filters, and camera operation, concentrates more on aesthetics. Actually, the technical and the aesthetic go hand in hand. Performance, an aesthetic phenomenon, cannot be discussed without the need for understanding technically how lighting and choice of camera lenses and camera angle can augment performance.

While many books have been written on the art of cel (hand-drawn) and computer graphics animation, very few have been devoted to stop-motion puppet animation. All animation techniques have their own idioms, though all share certain fundamentals in key pose, anticipation, follow-through, ease-in and ease-out, and so forth. Computer and cel animation provide the luxury of moving back and forth through the animation; one can edit, erase, move, cut, and expand or condense the animation itself in a nonlinear manner. This is not so for stop-motion animation. Considered an exclusively "linear" animation, stop-motion requires that the puppet go through its paces without interruption. This manual will explore the challenges and problems that this linear technique presents to the stop-motion animator.

The first half of this manual concentrates on the aesthetics of lighting and cameras as they pertain to the preparation of performance animation. The last half deals with the process of performance itself. Often, the most successful animation, like acting, relies on body language and facial expression as it relates to emotion. The great silent films stars relied on movement, facial expression, montage, and editing more than they relied on title cards to convey thought, emotion and story. One only need look at Buster Keaton's *The General* (1927) or Charlie Chaplin's *City Lights* (1931) to realize the power of body and facial play.

This power is available to the stop-motion animator. The aim of this book is to help the animator discover — getting in touch with his own inner actor — how to find the power and put it to work.

CHAPTER 1

"The Play's the Thing"

"The play's the thing wherein I'll catch the conscience of the king"
—*Hamlet* (Act 2, sc. 2), William Shakespeare

Characterization and performance interpretation (be it animation or live-action performance) finds its growth in story structure. This chapter will deal, in a cursory manner, with the elements of how traditional **narrative** film structure works.

A number of years ago I was a graduate student at a university. I brought to that faculty an idea for a narrative film project I was thinking about producing for my graduate thesis. Since I have an interest and specialization in animation, I chose the animation medium as a way of shooting the film. After I finished my proposal, a senior faculty member told me that he did not understand what I wanted to do. He went on to say that my idea was "too Disney," had already been done. What I found most surprising coming from a teacher was his statement that he knew nothing about animation and did not know how to advise me.

Directed to a younger student, this might have had rather serious repercussions. Fortunately, I was already into my forties and had seen enough of life's experiences to see the difference between constructive criticism and blatant personal prejudice directed from one individual to another. I told him that it was not necessary for him to know anything about animation, but that he should know something about filmmaking and story, because that was what I was, a filmmaker, and that I hoped he agreed. He did not, or chose not to. When it became clear that he and a few other faculty members were not going to support my endeavors academically and offer practical and constructive criticism, I left their program for greener pastures.

I share the above incident because it is a classic example of what I feel is, in general, much of academia and much of the art and filmmaking community's misguided view of animation: namely, that it is a technique, exclusive to itself, and has little or nothing to do with what is considered "normal" (i.e., live-action) filmmaking. I believe that this view is incorrect. Do not be misled into thinking that animation stands apart from the live-action medium. In the opinion of this author, it does not. The animation medium, like the live-action medium, is only a tool and by-product of the storytelling process. All roads, regardless of the process, move toward the same destination: to entertain, enlighten, and move an audience.

Story — The Idea

An old cliché in the motion-picture profession goes, "There are three things that make a great film: (1) story, (2) story, and (3) story.

What is a story? Where does it come from and how does one find inspiration for a story? Age-old questions to be sure, though it may be more appropriate to ask, "What makes a good story?"

Stories (the author is speaking of strictly fictional narrative form) have been around for thousands of years in one form or another. The ancient Greeks were very fond of telling stories, particularly plays, peopled with very emotionally driven and complex characters and situations.

Successful art, whether it is a novel, film, sculpture, painting, stage play or piece of music, does not happen overnight. It takes thought, planning and the willingness to say, "That doesn't work. Let me try something else." After living with something for six months, it is very difficult to be objective and to look at it with a critical and fresh eye. Being objective about one's own work of art is difficult, because if one has grown attached to something, it is very difficult to let it go, even if it is not serving the interest of the work. It may be a great idea, but is the idea serving the whole of the story? And where does one get a good idea anyway?

Contrary to some opinions, it is not particularly difficult coming up with an idea for a **plot**, because it is often drawn from our own personal life experiences and the people we know or have come across in our life's walk. All we need to do is look around and observe others' lives, as well as our own, as inspiration for material. Occasionally, an idea for a plot is to move one genre to another. *Star Wars* (20th Century–Fox, 1977) is, more or less, the western formula transplanted to the science-fiction genre, with sprinkles of mysticism. *Casablanca* (Warner Bros., 1942) is the story of a former freedom fighter whose female lover has left him, and who now has difficulty trusting and relating to other people, let alone developing another romantic relationship. *Citizen Kane* (RKO, 1941) is the tale of a wealthy man who had everything materially, but lost, or never truly had, that which was most precious to him: his youth and family. These are simple, though very real, commonplace issues in human drama that we all face and see on a day-to-day basis. The difficulty comes, of course, through written dialogue and performance to pull it off successfully. No easy task, but not impossible.

Many good stories are actually born of everyday situations and of characters who place themselves or unwittingly find themselves in extraordinary circumstances that they are not accustomed to dealing with (usually called the **conflict**). In fact, all one needs to do is look at the great narrative literature and films of history to see this happening. What one finds are stories that are peopled with relatively normal everyday individuals, but who must deal with abnormal or difficult circumstances. Audiences watching a play or film will readily attach themselves to a character if they empathize or understand that character's situation, particularly if they have been through it themselves (such as an alcoholic parent, a physical handicap, or shyness). The list is endless.

Take, for example, someone who is a commercial airline pilot in a dramatic film. Most people in the audience are not pilots, and as such, will not be able to relate to such a person on that level. However, being a pilot is not about being human. The character may be a pilot, but what the audience discovers as the story unfolds is that his wife is about to leave him for another man, or he has just discovered that he has terminal cancer and that this will probably be his last flight. Or his teenage daughter does not understand him and vice versa. Most audience members will not understand what it means to be a pilot and they probably would not care anyway, but some will certainly be able to identify with a person who is going through a divorce, has lost a loved one to cancer, or cannot relate to a teenaged child.

Of course, what the character does professionally can tie in to the situation. If he has cancer and is dying, perhaps he (for the first time in his life) comes to grips with the age-old question, "Why are we here?" which all of us have asked at one time or another. When he is above the clouds in his plane, he finally becomes aware of his mortality and views the beauty of nature in a way that he never saw, or at least had taken for granted for many years. In short, he finds himself. To illustrate further, if his wife is leaving him, he slips into mental illness and in despair may or may not decide to crash the plane, thus creating suspense. When the plane malfunctions (a mere malfunction, or divine intervention?), he is snapped from his depression and lands the plane safely. Everyone on board is rescued. And he himself is saved, both physically, emotionally, mentally, and probably most importantly, spiritually. Happy ending.

If we use one more illustration, his daughter is kidnapped and he suddenly rushes to her rescue with the ransom money, commandeering an aircraft illegally. The authorities demand that he land the plane immediately and surrender, but he refuses. He must first rescue his daughter within twenty-four hours before the kidnappers murder her. In the meantime, the authorities are trying to shoot him down because they don't know what his motives are. Double jeopardy, the stuff of thrillers. Or, there is a bomb on the plane and nobody knows about it except the audience. Or ... Get the picture? It can go anywhere.

Tapping into people's fantasies about who they would like to be is another way to connect the audience to your material. If, for example, one has fantasized about being a secret agent, one might enjoy reading a novel or watching a film about a do-good, globe-trotting spy. What must be injected, however, is a sense of humanness to the spy's character before anyone can become involved on an emotional level. He may be a globetrotting spy, but if he is a flawed character in a way that the audience member or reader is flawed (addicted to drugs, has a bad marriage, has a dark past, yells at his kids when he doesn't mean to, etc.), then the audience will be better equipped to identify with that person. Nobody can empathize with a perfect character, because nobody is perfect. Perfection is dull.

In his timeless novel *A Christmas Carol*, Charles Dickens created the moneylender Ebenezer Scrooge, a mean-spirited, miserly, and spiteful elderly man who has distanced himself in his autumn years from his fellow man and life in general. Dickens spends time in the early portion of the novel introducing Scrooge's personality to the reader. The reader never really knows how Scrooge got that way, just that he is so. They care little that he is a businessman. He could have been almost anything: a farmer, butler, whatever. Since Scrooge is a miser, the fact that he handles money lends to the situation a darkly comic irony. But almost every human on the face of the planet has at one time or another met or known someone who is angry, disdainful, stingy, selfish, or hurtful to others. Perhaps they were or are Scrooge themselves. As

Dickens' story unfolds, Scrooge is given a miraculous opportunity to review his life, past, present, and future, to see how it unfolded and how he got to his place in his life, and if he desires to remain there. The ending is, of course, literary legend.

In the William Wyler film *Ben-Hur* (MGM, 1959), we are introduced to two men during the time of Jesus: Judah Ben-Hur, a wealthy young Hebrew, and the Roman Massala, his childhood friend and now Roman officer. As the Romans prepare to occupy Jerusalem, Judah is torn between his lifelong friendship with Massala and his love and duty to the people of the Jewish nation and his heritage. When he chooses his people, Massala cuts his friendship with Judah and prepares to overtake the city. Judah is exiled and his family imprisoned. While audience members may not be Jewish or Roman, you can bet many, if not all of them, will understand what it feels like to lose a friend, or to feel prejudice and hatred, or to be bullied. You want your audience to understand and empathize what the person on-screen or in the novel is feeling and going through.

The Stanley Kramer film *The Defiant Ones* (United Artists, 1958) is, in essence, a theme and variation of the buddy idea that *Ben-Hur* uses, albeit in reverse: two convicts, one African American and the other a Caucasian, escape from prison. Chained together, they are forced to rely on one another for survival, even though racial prejudice cause them to despise one another. In an ironic twist, their chain becomes their redemption; forced to remain together, they begin to learn about one another and discover that they are both human, have the same human wants, and have experienced anger, loss, love, and whatever else it means to be human. When their chain is finally broken, the African American is told that he can make for the train through a swamp. When the Caucasian learns that the swamp is filled with quicksand, he races after his new friend in an attempt to warn him. In the final moments of the film, the two are reunited in each other's arms (a symbolic image of racial acceptance) as the sheriff's posse arrives to reclaim them for prison.

What does all this mean? It means this: If you give your character or characters problems and situations that all humans deal with daily, and if your writing and the actors' (live actors as well as animators) performances have depth and appear real, then people will almost certainly empathize and connect with the characters and story, regardless of the genre of the film. And once they connect, they will not want to leave until they see the outcome.

Let us now discuss a few aspects of narrative story structure.

Story Structure — Narrative Form

Traditionally, narrative structure uses plot as the spine, or central driving force, of the story. Within this plot can be (though not always) subplots, a conflict (almost always), central characters, secondary and tertiary characters, a **catalyst**, and an ending of some sort. Sometimes the term "minor character" is used, but I personally do not care to use this because it tends to cheapen the importance of the secondary characters' roles. All characters in a story have importance and contribute to furthering the story, else the writer would not have included them. Not only that, but also all characters, regardless of their screen or stage time, have motivation, give something, and desire something, thus fueling the plot.

Form and Content

Form deals with the actual structure of a work of art. **Content** is that material itself which makes up the work in question (the plot, for example). In Beethoven's Fifth Symphony, Fate knocking at one's door supplies the **content**, and its structure is the sonata form. Let us continue this example briefly as it applies to music because it shares its structure very closely to narrative story structure.

There are many types of form that composers have used for centuries to develop their works. During the classical era of music (the dates overlap various composers, but the period spans roughly 1750–1830), one of the more popular forms of music was the sonata (or sonata-allegro) form. Characteristic of

some of the instrumental works of Mozart, Haydn, early works of Beethoven, and their contemporaries, the sonata form is, in its most basic appearance, broken into three primary constituents:

1. **Exposition** — which introduces at least two different themes, which are in turn woven in one form or another throughout the entire composition.
2. **Development** — the central section of the work, primarily in its dramatic and emotional impact (fast, slow, loud, soft, as well as key changes).
3. **Recapitulation** — as its name implies, the recapitulation is material heard earlier in the exposition, with various modifications and changes at the whim of the composer.

The recapitulation is generally followed by a **coda**, which is a sort of elaborate flourish of notes that allows the musician to showcase his/her technical expertise and finish the work, followed by (hopefully) thunderous applause.

In short, form is used to provide a basic structure of the art in question, allowing for a sequence of events to take place. The form therefore acts as the building blocks of art, but in some situations, as deemed by the artist, things can be modified to allow for innovative and original ideas to take place, depending on the inventiveness and cleverness of the artist to create something new and refreshing. After all, rules are meant to be broken, provided that one knows how to break them.

The Three-Act Narrative Form

Traditionally, narrative motion pictures have generally relied on three-part narrative form to structure their screenplays. Broken down in its most basic outline, we find this:

1. Act One–Exposition(introduction of central characters, and establishing the plot and introduction of the conflict).
2. Act Two–Development (working out the conflict).
3. Act Three–**Resolution** or conclusion (happy, sad, or ambiguous ending).

Most narrative scripts (primarily film and TV) use this formula. One of the finest examples of scriptwriting I have seen (feature or otherwise) was a thirty-minute adaptation of the 1902 W.W. Jacobs short horror story *The Monkey's Paw* for television. A truncated description of the short story follows:

A middle-aged couple and their adult son live in a small house. A stranger comes by and offers them a mummified monkey's paw, claiming that it can grant them three wishes, but to be careful what one wishes for. The father wishes for two hundred pounds; the paw twists in his hand and he drops it to the ground in fear. The following day, the son walks off to work. Shortly, an employee of the son's company arrives to tell the parents that their son was killed in a horrible machine accident, his body twisted and crushed beyond recognition. As insurance compensation, the company is giving them two hundred pounds. A few days later, distraught and shaken, the father holds the paw again and wishes his son alive. Late that night, someone begins to knock incessantly at the front door. Thinking it is her son coming back from the dead, the mother attempts to unlatch the door as the banging becomes louder and more powerful, while the father frantically grabs for the monkey's paw. With one final wish, he wishes his son dead just as the mother opens the door to find no one there.

This nutshell description of the short story does not by any means do justice to the psychological terror that Jacobs builds as one reads along, but I list it here briefly to illustrate that its form appears to follow a three-act narrative.

1. The family inherits the monkey's paw (exposition).
2. The son is killed and the parents inherit the insurance money. The father wishes his son alive (conflict/development).
3. Something bangs on the front door and the father wishes his son dead (resolution — ambiguous).

There are various schools of thought concerning three acts versus one, two, or four or more acts when constructing a script story. There is no hard-and-fast rule. Some films (most notably Luis Buñuel's 1968 *Belle de Jour*, or some of the films of Quentin Taran-tino) jump back and forth in the narrative structure, play with time, or play with what is real and what is not. It may behoove the writer to simply begin writing and not concern himself with form per se. Successful art can often find its inspiration from simple improvisation, and one may find it a hindrance to the creative process if one is attempting to follow a set rule. However, newcomers to scriptwriting may find the three-act form easier to understand and deal with. Later, one can branch out to more complex forms or simply experiment.

CHARACTERS

A question often asked is, What drives a story: the characters or the plot? It is really both, working hand-in-hand to propel the story forward. A story can have one or more characters, though generally there is nearly always more than one. Humans are in constant contact with one another daily, and a film audience can much more readily identify with two or more characters relating on the screen. Even if you have only one human in your story, a nonhuman entity can play (symbolically/**metaphorically**) as a character against the human one. If a man is the only person on a deserted island, the island itself can play as a character. The elements can play as characters (wind, sea, fire, earth). Characters within a story can be anything: humans, animals, the elements, etc. In his novel *The Old Man and the Sea*, Ernest Hemingway uses the sea as one of his central characters. A storyteller is not limited to using just humans as characters. Indeed, in *Star Wars* (20th Century–Fox, 1977), writer-director George Lucas uses the Force as a central character (or plot-point, if you will) in developing the story. While the audience cannot see the Force as a physical entity, they can see its effect on the external world.

PLOT

Plot refers to the basic idea of the story and is the driving force of the narrative. Plots can be quite simple in nature or very complex. Many of the screenplays of director John Sayles rely on a complex character-driven narrative to propel the story. His characters are complex and, while seemingly unrelated to each one, nonetheless often cross paths and come into contact with one other at some point during the story. In his 1996 film, *Lone Star* (Sony Pictures/ Castle Rock Entertainment), Sayles creates the plot of the story: a twenty-five-year-old human skeleton, wearing a sheriff's badge, is found in the desert near a small Texas town. Local sheriff Sam Deeds is brought in to solve the mystery, and as he digs deeper into the case, he begins to find details of the murder and its possible association with his own father, a former sheriff, whose shadow Sam has been living in all his life. The story is rich in characterization, with characters linking to each other in one form or another.

However, one need not always pen such elaborations to create compelling stories. In the Robert Bresson film *A Man Escaped* (French, Gaumont/SNE, 1956), the audience is introduced to a young man who makes plans to escape from a Gestapo prison during World War II. There is little dialogue or ensemble interplay. Instead, Bresson uses shot composition (**mise-en-scène**), editing (montage), and the performance of the actor to convey inner thoughts and feelings while in his holding cell. The plot, which is based on a true-life incident of French resistance fighter Andre Devigny, is whittled to its bare essentials to startling effect. A young man is incarcerated in a Nazi prison and immediately makes plans to escape. The only tools at his disposal: whatever materials he can find in his cell and elsewhere, and his ingenuity. Taunting, suspenseful, and compelling, the film is a masterpiece of storytelling.

Plot is therefore the spine of the narrative, the core of the story that introduces the audience to the situation and plight of the characters.

CONFLICT

Once the exposition of the story has been showcased (which includes the introduction of the central characters and their situation), a conflict of some sort is introduced (usually at the conclusion of the first act) to give the story a dramatic edge and to propel it, thus keeping the story going.

As mentioned earlier, the plot of the film *Ben-Hur* deals with the friendship between the Hebrew, Judah Ben-Hur; and the Roman officer, Massala. The conflict occurs when Judah realizes that if he is to keep his close friendship with Massala, he must compromise his situation by turning his back on his Jewish heritage and fellow countrymen, and give in to the rule of the Roman government. When his mother and sister are arrested by Massala and imprisoned, Judah turns his back on Rome, which also means severing his friendship with Massala.

A study of the lust for power and wealth, and the madness it can bring, German filmmaker Werner Herzog's 1972 masterpiece, *Aguirre, der Zorn Gottes* (*Aguirre, the Wrath of God*, DVD distributor, Anchor Bay Entertainment), introduces us to a 17th-century band of mercenaries led by Spanish conquistador Gonzalo Pizarro, who is bent on locating El Dorado, the legendary city of gold in the Peruvian jungle. When it becomes apparent that the expedition must split up, Pizarro commands his officer Pedro de Ursua to continue into the jungle with de Ursua's own party. Among this group is the subordinate officer, Aguirre, a moody, almost sinister man who secretly desires power and wealth for himself. As the party continues on through the dense, virtually impenetrable jungle, they are set upon by hostile natives, sickness, death, and hunger. When the party slowly succumbs to despair, Aguirre, seeing his chance, murders de Ursua and makes himself leader of the group. The final moments of the film reveal Aguirre completely insane, as he shouts to the elements and the hundreds of small jungle monkeys swarming his raft about his divine role as "the Wrath of God." The resolution and lesson to be learned: Absolute power corrupts absolutely.

The plot of *Aguirre* deals with the search by a Spanish expedition for El Dorado and the political struggle for power within this group. The conflict occurs when de Ursua realizes Aguirre cannot be trusted and makes futile attempts to keep Aguirre from taking over and ultimately destroying everything they have set out to accomplish.

CATALYST

A relatively common technique of providing a change or twist in the narrative is the use of a catalyst. Filmmaker Alfred Hitchcock was fond of using what he referred to as the "MacGuffin." The MacGuffin itself is not necessarily of any intrinsic value, but the fact that it motivated his central characters to action certainly was. For example, in his film, *Notorious* (RKO Pictures, 1946), the discovery of the wine bottles filled with uranium ore in a Nazi basement provides the catalyst for American secret agent Cary Grant to be spurred into action and help vanquish the foes.

A catalyst is more or less the same thing as a MacGuffin. One might also think of it as a plot-point, something that occurs in the course of the story that provides a means of either keeping the characters moving toward their goal or deflecting them into another direction that they had not thought about earlier, but that benefits their own personal growth or situation.

RESOLUTION

As one might surmise, the resolution is the conclusion of the story. The conclusion may or may not be a happy one. In fact, it can be ambiguous. It can also be a bittersweet conclusion, such as the ending of the 1997 British drama *The Wings of the Dove* (Miramax/Renaissance Films), or a tragedy, as in the conclusion of the ancient Greek stage drama *Medea*.

The ending of any story is really dependent on what has transpired through the course of the narrative. Often, the ending writes itself, though it can also reflect the final decision as to what the writer deems appropriate to the plot and where the characters eventually find themselves.

CHAPTER 2

Motion-Picture and Digital Video Cameras

The art and craft of traditional cinematography deals, in part, with the art and science of using motion-picture cameras, lights, filters, light meters and lenses to capture, on film, images that will eventually be projected at 24 frames per second, to create the illusion of motion. This process also includes the cinematographer's creative alliance with the director and other individuals on the set who decide on the final creative and aesthetic (emotional) look of the film as the consumer in a movie theater will finally experience it.

With the advent of digital technology and computer-based editing and compositing software, the traditional photochemical process of film will someday (and probably in the not-too-distant future) become obsolete, at least from a commercial standpoint. Indeed, there are distinct advantages to shooting digitally:

1. Instant feedback of your shot sequence, to see if your footage is working (technically as well as aesthetically).
2. Ability to instantly upload filmed images into one's PC or Mac computer for editing and compositing of visual effects.
3. No need to pay for expensive dailies, and hence, considerable savings of actual production costs.
4. Quick and efficient streamline cutting of footage, once the footage has been transferred to the PC/Mac.

5. Smaller and lighter equipment, which makes location shooting much more accessible.

There are also distinct advantages of shooting on film:

1. Film has a softer look than video, and can create very subtle shadow and light nuances. **Saturation** and resolution are outstanding.
2. Film is a universal commodity. Studios, equipment and talent can be found virtually anywhere in the world. Because of this, a universal standard was created to keep motion-picture cameras, projectors and other cinematographic equipment relatively consistent from country to country. Video, on the other hand, has many formats to offer (½", ¾", mini DV, high 8mm, etc.), and as such, the difficulty of showing one's video production shot on, say, ¾" beta may not be readily available if it is shown in countries that do not have the proper equipment.
3. Most filmmakers just plain prefer shooting on film because that is how they were trained and they are already familiar with their tools.

The disadvantage of shooting digitally:

1. Image quality of digital video is not as good as film, but this gap is quickly closing.

The disadvantages of shooting on film:

1. The final composition cannot be seen until the film is actually developed and sent back for viewing (and dailies cost money).
2. Many different types of **ASA** (i.e., film sensitivity to light) emulsions require one to tailor the shoot to the ASA, requiring the loading and striking of film in the camera film magazine, which can eat up production time.
3. Shooting on film must first be scanned into a computer before it can be integrated to the digital environment. This also costs money.
4. Linear editing of film (such as on a flatbed editor) is considerably slower than nonlinear.
5. To preserve the original photographed negative, an interpositive print (IP) is made for the original negative, and from this IP a duplicate internegative (IN) is made. From this IN, positive prints are made which are used for film distribution to theaters. This is a buildup of three generations, which can compromise image quality.
6. Film loses some of its image quality when it is scanned and broadcast through TV stations and on out into the airwaves.

However, as digital video technology continues to evolve and improve, the newer, younger generation who is growing up on this technology will replace the previous generation, and within one or two future generations, digital video will become as commonplace as film. In all likelihood, it will replace film. The current trend of manufacturers using three-chip digital technology in their camera recording systems enables the camera to utilize three chips, one for each of the three primary colors— RGB (red, green and blue) or YCM (yellow, cyan, magenta), depending on the process used — to allow the camera to record color. This technology is not without its drawbacks, as considerable amounts of memory are needed to process such information.

CCD Digital Video Technology

Charge Coupled Device (CCD) sensor technology was originally developed at Bell Labs in the late 1960s by George Smith and Willard Boyle. Describing the current technology behind CCD in depth is beyond the scope of this manual, but a cursory description will be provided here. Suffice to say, it is at least twice the resolution of standard 35-mm motion-picture film, and in time, will go even higher.

A CCD is a light-sensitive sensory chip and can be found in digital cameras and scanners, among other technology. There are three primary technologies used to record pixel color with cameras using CCD technology:

1. Sequencing Color
2. Color Filter Arrays
3. Three-Chip Color

Sequencing Color calls for a color wheel using red, green, and blue filters to alternate in front of a CCD chip for each image exposure. As one might suspect, however, this can take considerable time, as each digital "frame" (or image) must allow for the wheel to rotate for each of the three-color exposures.

A *Color Filter Array* allows for a prism beam splitter to be introduced between the lens and three CCD chips. As light enters the prism, the three colors (RGB) are distributed to their respective chip, thus recording color. In some respects, this color separation principle is (in its theory at least) similar to the old three-strip photochemical process used by **Technicolor**. The Technicolor camera ran three black-and-white panchromatic strips of film through its intermittent movement (Fig. 2-1).

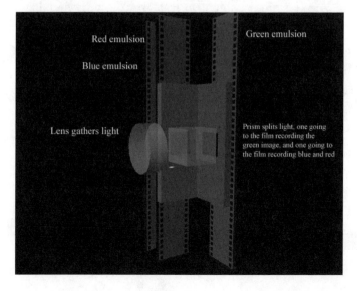

Figure 2-1

The camera used a beam splitter to separate the colors: red, green, and blue. The red light was sent to a panchromatic emulsion that was coated with red emulsion. The green light was deflected to a black-and-white panchromatic filmstrip. And the blue light was sent to black-and-white film stock that was coated with a red dye emulsion. When these three strips of film were later **contact printed** with blue-sensitive film stock, and later soaked with yellow, cyan, and magenta dyes (YCMs) to create the **release print**, a very dense, vibrant, saturated ultra-real color pallet was produced. This technology was particularly useful in musicals and fantasies, which created a hyper-real storybook illusion to transport the audience to exotic locales and into unreal situations, helping to suspend the audience's disbelief for one or two hours. In short, the technology changes (photo-chemical and digital), but the theory of color remains constant, never changing and always the same with respect to mixing and blending.

Three-Chip Color. Light entering a single CCD chip is split into three image planes, with each plane housing a color filter and a CCD chip. The camera can then pick up a color image by outputting the image planes in a synchronized fashion, from the three CCD image planes. In short, the switching of the three colors is instant, rather than one at a time (as in the case of the rotating color wheel in Color Sequencing).

The difficulty in the transition from film to video lies primarily in the fact that the film industry, having been in existent for over a century, has invested at least that many years through **R&D** as well as blood, sweat and tears in evolving and perfecting the motion-picture photochemical process. Once a successful time-proven process has been in place for so many years, having it change to another technology is extremely difficult and, at best, almost impossible. The amount of money it will take to change over to digital (both on the production and the exhibitor's ends) is considerable, though not impossible. With new technology comes the need to implement the equipment and train those who must run it. This change may be likened to the current trend in the automobile industry: as the world's resources in petroleum and oil begin to shrink, newer forms of energy must be drawn upon to fuel the automotive industry. Hydrogen and cell-driven electric cars may be the answer, but to have a multibillion-dollar-a-year industry change its tune overnight is easier said than done. The film industry is really no different.

Also, with the development of **HDTV** (High-Definition Television), TV broadcasting stations must commit to the financial and technical change-over of equipping their studios to receive such signals. Still, it is only a matter of time before HDTV becomes the mainstay of the broadcast image. However, as digital technology continues to improve and become more expedient financially and technically (with an emphasis on financially), more and more film studios will gladly embrace digital filmmaking.

Motion-Picture Cameras

As of this writing, motion-picture cameras are very slowly being usurped by digital cameras for motion-picture production (documentaries, features, shorts, etc.). As the technology of digital cameras improves, less reliance will be placed on film cameras. However, there is still a large amount of filmmaking that is being shot on film cameras, and this section will deal with film cameras, as well as a brief description of motion-picture film formats.

Motion-picture formats have a rich history of many types and sizes, makes and models. Suffice to say, the formats can be more or less lumped into four basic formats: 8mm, 16mm, 35mm, and 65mm.

As the reader can see, the format basically doubles as it gets larger. 8mm cameras were developed beginning in the 1930s and on through the 1970s for the general consumer who could not afford the more higher-end 16mm format. The 8mm format was relegated primarily to home films and amateur filmmaking. The format is still in existence, but few people use it, opting instead for the more easily accessible and instantaneous digital image.

Eastman Kodak developed 16mm film originally in the early 1920s for the everyday consumer. As the decades proceeded, 16mm film stock and cameras improved, and this format eventually found a niche in independent production and documentary film-making. In fact, modern-day 16mm cameras and equipment (such as Aaton, Bolex, Éclair, and Arriflex) are all state-of-the-art motion-picture cameras that offer superior quality when used properly.

Thirty-five millimeter film is the mainstay of theatrically released feature film, and has been for many decades. Whenever one goes to see a feature film in a local theater, they are watching a 35mm print. Some common 35mm cameras used in features include the Mitchell and Panavision cameras.

The larger format 65mm was used on Hollywood event films such as *Around the World in 80 Days* (1956), among others. These days, 65mm seems to be generally relegated to special-event theaters, such as IMAX. The size of the negative can drive production cost up considerably, which is why most feature film studios stay with 35mm. During shooting of 65mm, the film is run through the camera as a 65mm negative. However, during the inclusion of the soundtrack in postproduction, 5mm are added to the negative (2.5mm on each side of the film), to bring the format size up to 70mm. Therefore, the release prints are 70mm. The companies that specialize in this format are Todd-AO and Arriflex, among others.

In any photographic medium (still or motion picture), the larger the negative, the higher the saturation and resolution, and hence the cleaner the image. One only need compare a 35mm print shot with an SLR camera and an 8 × 10 print shot with a Hasselblad still camera to see this happen. The resolution of a digital image has nothing to do with the size of the camera and everything to do with the amount and size of pixels representing the color from the CCD sensors.

THE NECESSITY FOR FILM STEADINESS

A fundamental requirement of motion-picture filming is the camera's need to keep the film steady in the **aperture** while the film is running at twenty-four frames per second. In conventional still photography (such as in the use of an SLR camera), an image is taken only once and the film advanced to the next frame. In motion-picture photography, the camera is

designed to accommodate the exposure of twenty-four frames (images) every second. Once the film is processed and projected at twenty-four frames per second in a movie theater, the illusion of movement is created. But in order for this to occur properly, the film must be *exactly registered* from one frame to the next at all times during the twenty-four-frame cycle.

The basic components of the inner workings of an intermittent movement of a motion-picture camera include (Fig. 2-2):

1. **Pressure plate**
2. **Pull-down** claw (film transport claw)
3. 1 or 2 **registration pins**
4. Aperture (film plane)
5. **Shutter** (variable or capping)
6. Lens
7. Film emulsion

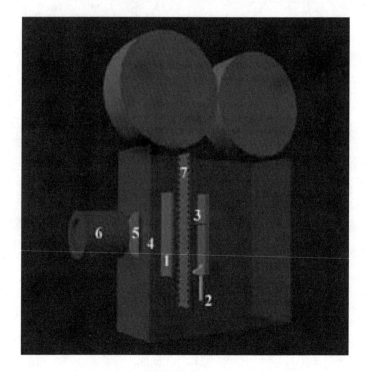

Figure 2-2

Registration pins are especially critical in animation cinematography, because each frame of film must be properly registered in succession through the film gate in exactly the same way. Any deviance of this may compromise the image during 24-frame projection and create "image weave."

During advancement of each frame of film, the following occur within the film gate:

1. A frame of film is resting in the film gate, with the registration pin engaged in the sprocket hole(s), keeping the film steady in the aperture for proper exposure.
2. To move the next unexposed frame into place, the shutter (which is between the lens and the aperture) rotates so that it blocks light from entering the aperture window, keeping the exposed frame from being overexposed.
3. The registration pin disengages from the sprocket hole, and the pull-down claw comes in and engages into the sprocket hole(s), pulling the film down until the next frame is advanced.
4. Once the next frame is registered in the aperture, the registration pin again engages in the sprocket hole, keeping the film rock steady in the gate so that the shutter can rotate around to allow light to enter for another exposure.
5. This process repeats every ¼th of a second (24 frames per second).

FILM EXPOSURE

The appropriate recording of any image during film exposure is determined by:

1. A light-capturing device (lens)
2. The amount of light entering the lens (f- or t-stop)
3. The opening size of the shutter
4. The amount of time (seconds/minutes/hours) one takes to record a frame of film
5. The ASA (ISO) (that is, the speed of the film; how sensitive it is to light)
6. The particular lights that are used (**key light, fill light,** sunlight, etc.)
7. **Gels** and filters

Lenses come in many shapes, sizes, and makes, depending on one's needs and visual requirement. The standard (prime) lens for 16mm filmmaking is a lens with a 25mm focal length. For 35mm cinematography, a lens with a focal length of 50mm is considered a normal lens. A **prime lens** is a lens that generally has a **fixed focal length** (as opposed to a variable zoom lens, which can have a variable focal length, such as 50mm to 120mm). Focal length is the distance between the center of a lens and the point at which an object is brought into focus: for our purposes, the film plane (that is, the surface of the film).

Lenses are also described as being fast or slow, or having a particular speed. This means that the light-gathering properties of a lens will either allow the lens to collect a great deal of light or very little light. This is useful if one is doing photographic effects, requiring long exposure times one frame at a time (slow lens), or low-light night/indoor scene cinematography (fast lens).

A lens also has on its barrel a ring that allows one to set the **f-stop** of the exposure. In photography, light is measured using a numeral system, ordered thus:

$$1.4 \quad 2 \quad 2.8 \quad 4 \quad 5.6 \quad 8 \quad 11 \quad 16 \quad 32 \quad \text{etc.} \ldots$$

These numbers can often be seen through the viewfinder of a reflex SLR camera, either running along the bottom or side of the aperture. These numbers can also be marked on the lens itself. A lens that is marked 1.6 on its ring indicates that that particular lens will stop down to an F 1.6. Paradoxically, the smaller the f-stop reading, the larger the iris or aperture, and the larger the f-stop number, the smaller the opening. If one has a large opening, more light will be allowed to enter and expose the film negative. Conversely, the smaller the opening, the less light will be allowed to enter.

THE SHUTTER

Shutters come in a few designs, a half-moon–shaped disc (Fig. 2-3), and the variable shutter, of which common for motion-picture cameras is the variable shutter.

In Fig. 2-3, the single rotating shutter rotates away

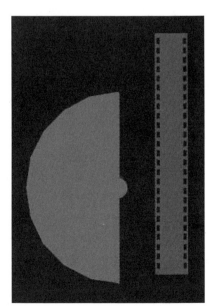

Figure 2-3

from the film and allows light to expose the negative frame. It then rotates in front of the film to prevent light from hitting the negative frame, while the pull-down claw advances to the next frame for exposure (Fig. 2-4).

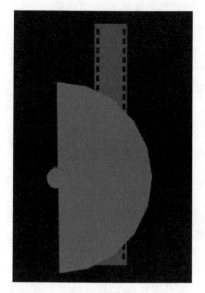

Figure 2-4

The variable shutter is comprised of two half-moon-shaped discs that move independently of one another on a rotating rod. By setting the shutter speed, one can rotate these discs so that the shutter can be set to either an open shutter (180-degree shutter) or completely shut (360-degree shutter).

Another type of shutter is the capping shutter. This shutter is particularly useful in visual-effects cinematography when shooting moving miniatures to create realistic blur effects. In stop-motion photography, each frame is always in sharp focus regardless of the speed of the puppet's motion, because the animator is stepping *between* frames to advance the puppet to its next position. As such, the puppet is always stationary when a frame is exposed. When the frames are projected at 24 frames per second, a stuttering or strobe effect is generated, making the motion appear unnatural.

Blur effects occur when an object is moving at a fast speed, such as a horse galloping. When each frame of the film is inspected after the film is developed, one can see that the legs of the horse are blurred. But when the frames are projected at 24 frames per second, a semblance of fluid motion is achieved. You can actually see this phenomenon occur in real life by moving your fingers in front of your eyes as fast as they can. Eventually, the speed of the hand will go beyond the ability of the eye to register a single finger with acceptable clarity, and the fingers will appear to be meshing together (Fig. 2-5).

Figure 2-5

The same holds true for rotating fan blades. If the fan is rotating at a slow enough speed, one can follow each individual blade around. As it goes faster, following one blade becomes increasingly difficult, until the blades are moving so fast that they blur together.

Before the advent of contemporary high-end, photo-real computer-generated imagery, spaceships were usually photographed as miniatures, which were either flown on wires in real time or shot as stop-motion animation. In the middle to late 1970s and on through the early 1990s, motion-control cinematography, in conjunction with blue-screen traveling matte work, was a means to impart more realistic motion to miniatures (*Star Wars*, 1977, *Close Encounters of the Third Kind*, 1977).

MOTION-CONTROL CAMERAS

Motion control is a process in which a motion-picture camera is externally motorized to create multiple passes of the camera for exact repeatability (Fig. 2-6).

Since visual effects process photography requires the use of many different elements that have been shot separately, exact repeatability is essential if all of the individual elements are to come together as one shot. A specialized platform is designed so that the camera can be run up and down on a track. Usually, a boom arm comes off of the track platform and

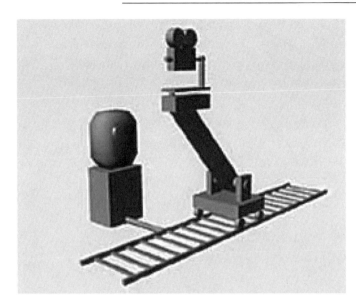

Figure 2-6

the camera is in turn connected at the end of this boom arm. This arrangement allows the camera to move forward/backward (track), side-to-side and up and down (boom arm), and the smaller platform that the camera rests on at the end of the boom also allows for pan, rotate, tilt, pitch and yaw, and all at the **camera nodal**. This then, enables the camera operator to move the camera in any way. A model spaceship is positioned on a blue pylon support in front of a blue screen (during the keyout process of **traveling matte** work, the pylon will disappear and the model will appear to be hovering in space). Since the model is remaining stationary on its pylon support, the camera motion actually creates the illusion that the ship is moving. Once a stationary background (star field) is composited with the moving spaceship via the blue screen, the illusion created is that the spaceship is moving past the camera, when in fact it was the camera that was moving. The entire motion-control rig runs electronically, enabling each axis of movement to be recorded on a magnetic or digital storage device. A capping shutter can take special advantage of this arrangement, because while the camera is moving in real time, the cap can flip up to allow for the exposure of a frame of film. But because the camera is actually moving past the model at such a slow speed, a blur effect is created on the negative. Once the film is projected 24 frames per second, a more realistic movement is imparted to the motion of the model. A theme and variation of motion con-

trol was employed in the 1983 film *Dragonslayer*, to create a more realistic moving dragon. A stop-motion puppet of a dragon was externally moved via rods attached to its feet, body and wings. The rods were attached to motors and the position of the rods was recorded on a computer. The animator would design his animation by moving the puppet through its steps single frame. Once the animation positions were recorded, the puppet was moved back to its starting point and the computer would push the rods to the next frame position that had been recorded by the computer. As the puppet was moving, the shutter would record the blur. This process was later abandoned due to its intense complexity and for all intents and purposes, has been replaced commercially by photo-realistic and full-motion computer-generated creatures.

ASA refers to the actual sensitivity of film emulsion to light, and stands for *American Standards Association.* While this association is now called the American National Standards Association (ANSI), the term ASA is still almost universally used when describing film speeds in the industry and on the set. Another rating used in Europe is DIN (Deutsch Industrie Norm). Both are described at length in the American Cinematographer Manual (see reference page at the end of the manual for publisher information). The smaller the ASA number, the less sensitive the film is to light. The higher the number, the more sensitive the film is to light. Therefore, a film stock with an ASA of 25 will be much less susceptible to light as a film stock with an ASA of 200, and hence requires more light to record an image. Lower ASA film speeds are very good for outdoor photography and for visual effects process photography. In motion-control cinematography, the camera is moving slowly on its track. As such, longer exposures are possible for each frame of film, so higher-speed film is generally not necessary. Indeed, in miniature photography, a visual effects cinematographer often needs to stop down his/her lens to either 16 or 32 (sometimes even lower) in order to hold **depth of field**. But the higher the number, the smaller the f-stop. Because of this, one often needs a great deal of light to reach the negative. One can use a higher ASA, but the higher the ASA, the more likely one is to obtain grain buildup. The alternative is to use a lower ASA and photograph frames with a longer exposure time for each frame.

Because of its greater sensitivity to light, high-speed film is good for indoor or night photography. However, high-speed film is generally susceptible to buildup of grain. The choice of film speed is determined largely by experience and the knowledge gained in how certain ASA is affected by light and filtering.

CHAPTER 3

Light and Lighting Basics

Cinematography is a difficult and complex art that requires the wedding of the technical tools of the cinematographer's trade to an aesthetic and artistic sensibility. While cinematography certainly requires technical know-how to achieve its end, cinematographers will sometimes speak of using a "painterly" effect. If they seek a soft, light effect, they may mention the golden age of Dutch painting and the work of the 17th century painter Jan Vermeer (1632–1675). The French cinematographer Henri Alekan (*Beauty and the Beast*, 1946) drew much inspiration from Vermeer's paintings as well as the works of the earlier Italian painter Michelangelo Caravaggio (1571–1610), whose works reflect strong, dramatic contrasts of light and shadow. Because of this, some cinematographers occasionally use the term "painterly" when describing their take on lighting a shot. Indeed, they will often explain how they "paint with light," as a painter will use brush and oils to create mood, atmosphere, shade, and value to their paintings.

What Is Light?

While light is not completely understood, there are at least two theories that can explain certain aspects of the makeup of light: wave theory, and particle theory. Physics defines light as charges of electromagnetic radiation *waves* that travel through space (vacuum) at 186,000 miles per second, and almost as fast as it moves through atmosphere. Light travels through water a bit slower. The speed of light is therefore contingent on the density of the matter it is traveling through.

Once light rays hit a surface and is **reflected** to our eyes, a chemical reaction occurs in which the optical properties of our eyes take the information and relay it to our brain, enabling us to perceive color and shadow (and thus see form and shape), so that we can perceive the external world in three dimensions (height, width, and depth). Color is seen when the surface of an object absorbs all light waves except the wave of the color in question, which is reflected back to our eyes. We can see a red car because the only light wave being reflected to our eyes from the surface of the car is the wave corresponding to the color red. The surface absorbs all other wavelength colors. Therefore, the frequency of a light ray will determine its **hue** (pure color).

There is an extremely wide range of electromagnetic energy occurring in the universe, and this is referred to as the **electromagnetic spectrum** (Fig. 3-1). Humans see only a fraction of this range, which is the visible spectrum. All other waves are invisible to the eye.

The Visible Spectrum

A prism divides light into a rainbow of colors: red, orange, yellow, green, blue, indigo and violet (Fig. 3-2). If these colors are projected through another prism, white light will emerge from the other side.

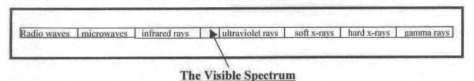

Figure 3-1

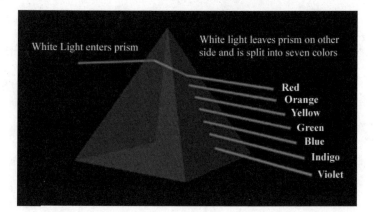

Figure 3-2

Light wavelengths are measured in millimicrons (abbreviated as mµ), and a millimicron is one millionth of a millimeter. A wavelength of 650–700mµ equals the color red, and a wavelength of 600mµ is orange. Blue is generated from a wavelength of 500mµ, and so on. As noted in Chapter 1, the three primary colors of light are red, green and blue (as opposed to the three primary colors of paint, which are yellow, red, and blue). When red, green and blue are overlapped, their complementary colors are generated: **Yellow** (overlapping red and green), **Cyan** (overlapping blue and green), and **Magenta** (overlapping blue and red, creating a purplish red), or Y-C-M for short. (Remember the Technicolor illustration from the previous chapter, and its use of YCMs as dyes to generate color from the three panchromatic emulsions?) And at the center of where the three colors overlap is white.

How Objects Are Affected by Light

Rays of light travel in straight lines. However, certain things occur when light hits an object. Not all objects have the same density and surface shape,

which affect the angle of light rays. For example, if an object enters a sheet of glass, the light rays will be bent (**refracted**), but when it exits the other side, it will come out at the same angle it originally went in, and is thus **transmitted**. If light rays strike an object that causes the rays to bounce away, the rays are said to be reflected. And if an object takes in the light rays, not allowing the light to be transmitted or reflected, the rays are **absorbed** into the object's surface (sort of like a benign black hole). The light does not come out of the other side of the object (Fig. 3-3).

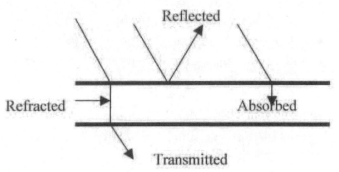

Figure 3-3

If a light is allowed to shine directly onto the surface of an object, the light may become too harsh or cause unnecessary **specular** highlights if the object has a shiny surface. To make the light appear softer, it can be diffused. In the case of diffusion, the light is being allowed to hit a rough surface, such as a piece of Styrofoam (Fig. 3-4).

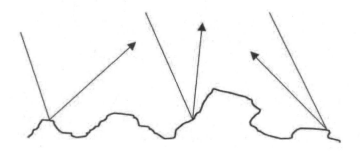

Figure 3-4

An example of diffusion that exists in real life would be an overcast day. The clouds, acting like a gigantic curtain, block out the sun's light rays and produce little to no shadow.

Diffusion material comes in basically two types:

1. Spun on a roll
2. White diffusion plastic, **semitransparent** and **opaque**

An object that is its own light source is considered to be self-luminous, such as a light bulb, the sun, a candle flame, etc. These objects tend to illuminate their surroundings, affecting other objects by having them reflect the luminous object's light rays that fall on them (that is, the illuminated body).

There is no substance that can be seen through completely (such as the invisible man) without our knowing it is actually there. However, there are many substances that do have a certain amount of "see-throughness" (such as glass, animation acetate cels, ice, and water). Objects such as these allow light rays to enter them and then exit via transmission, and are said to be transparent (Fig. 3-5).

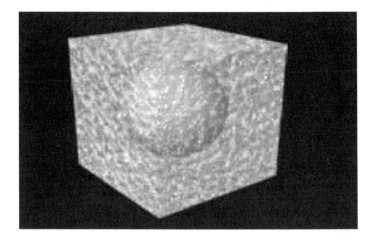

Figure 3-6

Figure 3-5

We refer to objects that have a frosty or semitransparent surface as **translucent** (Fig. 3-6).

This is because some light rays are being sent through and exited via transmission, but other rays are being diffused and reflected back. And if there is an object within the object being illuminated, the internal object will appear ambiguous, though it will have some sort of shape that is not easily discernable. Materials such as this would include frosted glass and ice cubes. A famous film example of using translucency to create psychological tension can be seen in the science-fiction horror film *Alien* (20th Century–Fox, 1979). As an astronaut inspects what appears to be some sort of large

translucent alien eggs inside a crashed derelict spaceship on a remote planet, he begins to see within it a strange shape that begins to move. He is able to see, to a limited degree, the object within because the outer surface of the egg is translucent. This plays very well on the audience's psychological feelings because, like the astronaut, they do not know what is inside the egg. Friend or foe? Their worst fears are realized when a loathsome parasitic creature bursts from the egg and attaches itself to the astronaut's face, forcing him to play host to an even more terrible foe later in the film. The director took advantage of transparency and effective lighting to convey a most loathsome alien terror, enabling him to mount growing suspense.

Finally, the opaqueness of an object indicates an object's inability to reflect light within itself, thus absorbing all light rays except the rays of the color that it is, thus making it appear solid (Fig. 3-7).

Figure 3-7

Let us now explore the concept of lighting a shot, and the terminology of the various equipment used in illuminating characters and scenes.

Fundamentals of Lighting

CREATING DEPTH IN A TWO-DIMENSIONAL ENVIRONMENT (THE MOTION-PICTURE IMAGE)

A motion picture is, in effect, a series of still images that are projected in quick succession to create a semblance of fluid naturalistic motion via the phenomenon of **persistence of vision**. The fact that they are still photographic images, however, indicates that the image we are seeing is not a three-dimensional environment; it is flat.

The real world exists in three dimensions (height, width, and depth), but the photographic image (including a motion-picture frame) is two-dimensional (height and width). If we are standing in an apple orchard and fix our gaze on an apple hanging off a branch, and then move our head to the left or the right, we change our visual perspective on the apple and will begin to see around its side. We can see what is behind it as well as our view on the background shifts (**motion parallax**). If we are looking at this same apple in a photograph or on a movie screen, we cannot shift our view or see around it, because the apple exists in a two-dimensional environment (in this case, the photograph or movie frame); it is simply a recorded image. How, then, can a cinematographer create the *illusion* that a two-dimensional image has depth even though, literally, it doesn't? A challenging paradox. And since this book deals with the lighting of stop-motion puppets and miniature sets (themselves existing in real-world three dimensions), understanding proper lighting for this is extremely important. Let's explore the process.

There are a number of reasons why we perceive shape, form, and depth in our three-dimensional world. Because we have two eyes, our brain is able to discern a **stereoscopic** view of three-dimensional space. If a person gazes before him/her, then closes one eye, opens it again and closes the other eye, the environment will shift slightly to one side (right or left). This is a phenomenon called **spatial parallax view** and is integral in allowing us to experience the dimension of depth. Even if we close one eye, we can still see depth to some degree. This is somewhat due to the interplay of light and shadow.

A sphere is round but it also has depth. Primitive objects (spheres, cubes, cones, rectangles, and columns) all have depth as well as form and shape. Primitive shapes exist in great abundance in the real world. For example, an arm can be thought of as two columns that are attached to one another at the elbow (a column is round like an arm, but also has length). A head is a sphere, and a torso can be a cube. Breaking down real-world objects into their most basic shape components can assist the artist in creating the shape of an object (this is one of the fundamental approaches to computer graphics modeling) (Fig. 3-8).

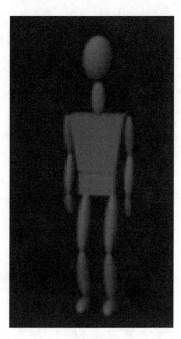

Figure 3-8

However, depth (or at least the illusion of depth) will not be perceived until the following happen:

1. Light rays must hit the surface of an object (flat or three-dimensional) and reflect the necessary wavelengths back to our eyes, so that we can see its color or grayscale.
2. The object must cast a shadow onto another object or surface, so that it can be set apart from its surroundings,

and/or:

3. The object must have a shadow on itself to sculpt the shape and thus fill out the form.
4. Since humans tend to be attracted to light, an object can be set apart from its background by making the background darker by creating contrasts of light and dark.

Movement through Space Creates Depth in the Two-Dimensional Medium of the Motion Picture

Photography and cinematography are both concerned with lighting objects and/or a set to optimize a certain look and/or feel. Unlike photography, however, cinematography affords the added plus of literally objects moving through space over time, helping to create a sense of depth.

In the following figure, a ball sits on the floor (Fig. 3-9).

Figure 3-10

Figure 3-9

Well thought-out design in painting, sculpture, and photographic imagery provides the viewer with subjective, kinetic movement. In the case of a motion picture, however, movement becomes almost purely objective. We see a ball as it slowly rolls toward us. As it does, it increases in size as it comes closer. The change in size (over time) of the ball reinforces our affirmation that the ball is coming at us from a certain distance from where it was originally. In addition, the lines in the floorboards help to convey motion as they travel toward the viewer in perspective, receding into the distance at an invisible vanishing point (Fig. 3-10).

Since the moving image is still a two-dimensional medium, film directors are continually thinking of ways to play the action in the frame to optimize the illusion of depth.

There is also another (and probably more important) aspect of creating depth in an image, and that is with shadow. Light and shadow must be used in tandem to create depth. They are inseparable. Without shadows, we cannot perceive the shape or form of an object. Shadows have density as well. One shadow may be extremely dark, while another might be on the gray side. One can think of the density of a shadow as a certain level of grayness, though shadows can certainly have color as well. The human eye can perceive over 7,000 colors in the visible spectrum.

Notice the marble against a wall background in Fig. 3-11.

Figure 3-11

Since the marble is not casting a shadow on the wooden wall behind it, we cannot tell how far it is from the background. As a result, we cannot sense much depth. Nor do we really know how large the sphere is; it could be one millimeter in diameter, or one thousand miles in diameter. Spatial relationships and shape familiarity are, hence, critical in determining size as well as distance from one object to another.

Allowing the marble to cast a shadow onto the background surface helps to suggest that it may be quite close to the background, but again, it does not tell us how large the marble and background actually are (Fig. 3-12).

Figure 3-12

The more objects we have in the scene, and if they progressively recede one from the other, we are not only telling the viewer that the objects are going off into the distance, but we are also implying that the background might be quite far away. However, unless the background is something terrestrially specific, the background can be any distance from us.

Another phenomenon is called **scattering**, and is never more evident than in the evening. When there is considerable material in the air, such as smoke, water condensation (fog), or dust, the light from street lamps, car headlights, or spotlights will shine among the material, which will in turn expose the light rays as they travel through space. The light waves are scattered in a random manner, falling, bouncing, and diffracting within the particles. This creates the beams of light that we see. Something related to this is **atmospheric perspective**.

ATMOSPHERIC PERSPECTIVE

This fall-off of color and definition as objects recede into the far distance is referred to as either **atmospheric perspective** or aerial haze, and they mean the same thing. Atmosphere is comprised of dust and/or water molecules (especially the air that is closest to the ground, where sky, water, and land meet and mix more easily). The particles in the air scatter light in all directions, and it is this scattering that causes a hazy effect.

A perfect example of observing atmospheric perspective is when viewing a mountain range. If you were walking through the Teton mountains of the Pacific Northwest, you would notice that the mountains closest to you have more textural detail, with plenty of dark shadows and color, than the ones farther away. As the mountains get farther away, there is a drop not only in texture of the mountain terrain, but also a shift in colors. Textures become less distinct, and things begin to shift toward the blue spectrum, including the blacks. This is because the dust, fog, and/or smoke that fills the air closest to us is within an area of land that is quite small (say, a 15- or 20-foot distance). Farther off into the distance, however (say, 20 miles or farther), we are able to view a greater area of land, but in doing so, we also must gaze through the immense amount of particles in the air that covers that distance. Hence, aerial haze becomes more distinct if we must see through a considerable distance of land and the representative particles (Fig. 3-13).

Figure 3-13

For atmospheric perspective to occur, the following must be affected:

1. Brightness
2. Contrast
3. Saturation
4. Clarity

A mountain in the distance is lit by the sun and as such reflects light waves back to our eyes, so that we can see the mountain. However, the sun also lights the dust and water particles in the air. So, not only are we seeing the light from the mountain, but the light coming from the particles as well. This causes the view to become **brighter** than it normally would be if the mountain were viewed closer, where the amount of particles in the air is less dense due to the mountain being closer.

For it to be seen, an object must have some degree of reflectivity as well as a certain amount of light falling onto its surface, so that darks can be observed. But in the case of our distant mountain, the light is scattered in the air particles. This cuts down on **contrast**, and little to no blacks are generated. Provided that there are closer mountains with some degree of shadow, these shadows will offset the haze of the distant mountains and a contrast of light and shade will be produced, helping to create the illusion of depth.

Haze also affects the **hue**. Hue is a color in its purest form and is completely saturated. If a mountain has a rich surface hue of green, the light reflecting off the green mountain surface must be reflected through the particles in the air as well. Once the green wavelength of the mountain surface mixes with the air particles and is diffused, the hue changes color and is desaturated, falling more on the bluish side. This breakdown in hue aids in the illusion of depth, provided that other mountains closer to the viewer have richer hues.

The combination of contrast and diffusion caused by the air particles breaks down the clarity (or sharpness) of the scene, giving the distant mountains a soft, fuzzy appearance. This "mushing" effect also enhances a sense of depth if closer objects are better defined.

Outstanding examples of visual effects using aerial haze technique as applied to stop-motion animation effects and miniature work can be seen in the mechanical walkers sequence in the 20th Century–Fox film *The Empire Strikes Back* (1979), and in the miniature work of *The Lord of the Rings* trilogy (2001–2003). A simple solution for creating atmospheric perspective with miniatures is to introduce bridal veil between the miniature and the camera.

In the case of lighting for interior miniature sets, aerial haze will not be a factor (unless, of course, the character is looking out of a window at a miniature landscape that goes off to infinity).

If we have spheres floating in outer space, we assume that the background is going off into infinity because we know that stars are light-years away and that space (as we currently understand it) is unending. We can see the spheres because the sun is lighting it. In this case, the sun is an infinite light source.

If three spheres are receding into distant mountains, we understand this distance because we are familiar with the fact that mountains are huge but they are also a finite distance away. What also aids the illusion that the spheres are receding toward the mountains, is a gradual fall-off of color and textural definition on the mountains themselves, as well as the spheres. Familiar shapes (including humans) are therefore necessary for us to perceive how far one object is from another (Fig. 3-14).

Figure 3-14

Forced Perspective

In Figure 3-15, both marbles appear to be side by side, sitting on the same imaginary ground level.

Figure 3-15

In fact, they are the same size, but the marble on the right has been moved farther away from the viewer than the one on the left. At this camera angle, there is no spatial relationship that can help us determine depth between the two. How can we illustrate depth here? This camera angle is allowing us to utilize **forced perspective**.

By moving the camera angle slightly up, we reveal the trick and show that one marble is actually farther away (Fig. 3-16). And if the farthest marble casts a shadow on the background, we know that it is

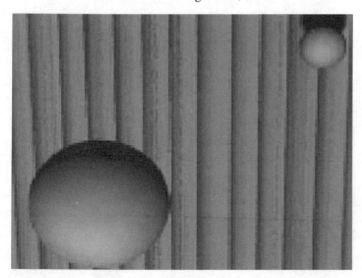

Figure 3-16

quite close to the wall, while the foreground marble must be quite far from the wall because it is not casting a shadow.

Volts, Amps, and Watts

When using film lights in one's house, there are a few things one needs to be aware of:

The electricity that comes from the outside line and into one's home outlet is approximately 120 volts (a circuit). All lights (movie, household incandescent, etc.) are rated at 120 volts.

Within a building (house or studio) is a junction box that houses all of the necessary fuses to monitor the amount of wattage that is being drawn on that particular circuit. Each fuse inside a junction box is generally 20 amps for any single circuit, and every 10 amps equals about 1,000 watts. So, for every 20 amp fuse, one can run about 2,000 watts; this means that one can run two 1-K lights off any single outlet, *provided* that no other appliances are on that circuit. Otherwise, you will short the fuse, and any electrical appliances that are on that circuit will fail (microwave oven, computer, washer/dryer, life-support system, etc.).

If you are unsure of what room is on what circuit, you can pull or turn off each fuse in the junction box and see what in your home/studio is deactivated. The fuse can then be labeled, indicating what light switches and appliances are on that circuit.

Types of Lights

While there are many shape variants of the three primary types of motion-picture lights available to the cinematographer, the three types used by the cinematographer for illuminating a scene and/or object are:

1. **Infinite Light**
2. **Point Light**
3. **Spotlight**

The choice of light is determined largely by how one needs to light the set, and what effect the director is after. One of the most common supplier of lights in the motion-picture industry is the Mole-Richardson Company. This company provides quartz-incandescent lights and their variants—light kits, flood lamps, fresnel lamps, etc.—to suit the needs of even the most discriminating cinematographer.

The ***infinite light*** is a direct light source that is powerful enough to light an exterior in a 360-degree radius, such as the sun. On a cloudless, noontime day, the sun will cast very harsh shadows. On a cloudy overcast day, the light will become **ambient**; that is, very few shadows will become apparent in your scene, and as such, the scene will look somewhat flat and lifeless. A good way to deal with ambient light is to look for distinct textures and color (or value, if shooting black and white) within the scene that stand out from the rest of the objects, and emphasizing those against the more plain-looking objects.

A point light is a light that is its own source light, such as a candle flame or a light bulb. All light rays from a point light will emanate in all directions from the source.

A ***spotlight*** (such as a ***flashlight***) is a light that enables one to place a concentrated beam of light into a specified area. Generally, the spotlight has a number of **barn doors** attached to the front of the light housing: one for the bottom, two on each side, and one at the top. These doors are opaque black and hinged, enabling the lighting person to move them up and down or side to side. By doing so, one can direct light into a specific area of the set. Spotlights are very useful for punching certain areas of the set with light, so that they will stand out in the scene. Since they are focused lights, they have a **cone angle** that allows the cinematographer to place the lights in any area of the set.

The most common lights for photographing dimensional animation effects work include:

1. Inky light
2. Baby light
3. Junior light
4. Senior light

These lights, with the exception of the senior, are small (particularly the inkies, which are very small), but because they are so petite, they can fit very well into stop-motion tabletop spaces, spaces that can generally be quite small and cramped. All of these lights are capable of taking bulbs that are balanced for 3,200 degrees Kelvin. A baby light is marked as 1K. In this case, K does not mean Kelvin, but rather the wattage of the bulb, with K meaning kilo, or thousandths. If a baby light is 1K, then it is 1 kilowatt (or 1,000 watts). A junior light uses 2K (2,000 watts) and a senior is 5K (5,000 watts). A baby can also accommodate a 500-watt bulb, provided it has the correct adapter.

Seniors, being a larger light, are sometimes used as a key light source when lighting the overall scene. The smaller lights are then used to create fills where necessary.

The Color Temperature of Light

Color temperature is a light's ability to give off a certain hue (color) when heated to a certain centigrade, and is measured in Kelvin units. This process of measuring the temperature of light was discovered by the 19th-century British scientist, Lord William Kelvin, and was so named after him. Kelvin discovered that if one burns any kind of material, that material would give off a certain color, depending on how hot (the temperature) it burns. By heating carbon to 3,200 degrees centigrade, Kelvin discovered that it gave off an almost white glow, and it is 3,200K that became the norm for suggesting daylight in cinematography. Therefore, most lights used in motion-picture cinematography are balanced for 3,200K, enabling them to burn white. Actual direct sunlight during the day (typically at around noon) has a color temperature of approximately 5,600K.

However, the incandescent filament of a light bulb (such as what is used in one's home) has a color temperature of roughly 2,600K when it heats. This would be unacceptable for indoor cinematography because its color temperature is lower that the required 3,200K for white light, instead giving off a green/pale-yellowish color.

Exposure Meters

Light meters are used to take measurements of light that is either being sent to the object being lit (from the light source) or to measure the amount of light coming from the object (reflected from the object). The **incident light meter** measure lights falling onto a subject, and is placed between the object being lit and the camera lens, with the meter's light-sensitive plastic dome (called the lumisphere) pointing toward the lens. Because the lumisphere is curved, it is able to take in most of the light that is falling on the subject. This meter has the following scales built into it (Fig. 3-17A):

1. Footcandle scale
2. Aperture value scale
3. Film ASA/ISO scale
4. Aperture scale
5. Stopper button
6. Shutter speed scale
7. Dial scale
8. Dial ring
9. Scale mark
10. Lumisphere
11. Memo pointer

Let us build a simple scenario for lighting a shot. You are shooting an interior scene with a shutter speed of 60, and the ASA speed of your film is 100. Move the ASA/ISO selector dial until it is set for 100. Next, place the meter before the subject and point the lumisphere toward the camera lens. Push the stopper button until you see the red needle move in the plastic window. If the needle points to, say, 4 on the aperture scale, look just above the aperture scale at the footcandle scale. The number 80 is above the 4. Your scene is 80 footcandles. Now, rotate the dial ring until the number 80 on the *interior* footcandle scale lines up with the black triangle. Once these two numbers are aligned, look at the shutter scale at the number 60 (your shutter speed). Just below the 60 is the aperture scale. The number 2 is below the number 60. The number 2 therefore indicates that you must set your lens aperture to 2.0 to photograph your scene.

Another type of meter is the **spot meter**. This meter measures a narrow bandwidth of light and as such is ideal for subjects that are within a small area of light (as in a spotlight, for example). Usually, the subject is quite far away from the camera, and because it is so far, an incident meter isn't useful because it needs to be right on the subject to take a proper reading for the exposure. The spot meter, however, will measure this light from a distance, enabling the cinematographer to set an appropriate exposure.

Key and Fill Light

Some cinematographers prefer not to label lights with particular names, though many use various terminologies when describing lights in creating a lit scene. For the purposes of this book, we will discuss lights as having specific functions.

A key light is generally the "lightest" light on the set. A key light might be thought of as a light that illuminates the predominant area of the set and/or object. The key enables the viewer to see the object in question, but a key by itself does not necessarily give the object an aesthetic sensibility. The fill light aids in that.

Without a fill light, an object lit with a key can appear flat and dull. Because of this, it is a good idea to introduce a light to fill in the shadows, allowing one to soften the shadows of the subject(s) and the set.

A **rim light** enables one to give the object a slight highlight around the edge of the object (Fig. 3-17B). Notice how the outer edge of the skeleton has a shiny glow, helping to offset it from the dark background.

Figure 3-17A

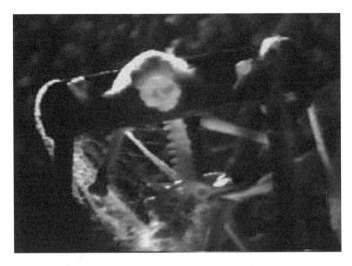

Figure 3-17B

This is very useful particularly if the object and background share a similar hue and shade.

One can have as many key and fill lights as one wishes. The trick, however, is to give the set and characters their own opportunity to come away from the background, and the only real way to do this is to work with the density of the shadows that are cast by the object(s) and creating a sense of perspective between objects by framing the shot, so that objects are displaced from one another in space.

Filters (Color and Neutral Density)

Color is an integral part of our everyday experience, and we are (consciously or unconsciously) affected by color emotionally. Red imparts a sense of heat and passion (red cars infer fast cars, warm red light can imply eroticism, etc.) while blue infers a callousness or coldness (ice cubes, emotional distance, etc). As such, the color spectrum carries with it our own emotional feelings. However, a lack of overt color in a film can suggest an emotional detachment, ambiguity, or sense of foreboding and thus work to the film's advantage, as in the 1991 thriller *The Silence of the Lambs*. The director, working with the cinematographer, chose to bathe the look of the film with muted color tones, which helped to emotionally heighten the dark, horrific plot of the story: An FBI agent must apprehend a murderer before he kills again, and the only

person who may know the killer's identity and who can help the agent is a brilliant physician who is an equally deranged psychotic incarcerated for murder and cannibalism. At the opposite end of the spectrum, the makers of the 1938 MGM fantasy classic *The Wizard of Oz* filled their scenes with a rich, full palette of colors to heighten and augment the childlike storybook feel of the narrative.

Generally, pure light that comes from either the sun or an artificial light will not adequately interpret that scene's color scheme. Because of this, the cinematographer must rely on various filters and gels to create a color scheme that will work for the given shot. There are many different filters and gels to suit the needs of virtually any situation. Among the most common types of filters are the Harrison and Harrison series. Filters alter the way a color is recorded on film, and thus actually changes the color temperature of the light. Neutral density filters, on the other hand, allow the cinematographer to reduce the camera's f-stop without compensating color temperature, such as if the scene is too bright and needs to be stopped down. Filters are generally placed in front of the lens of the camera, while gels tend to be placed over a light source.

Lighting Technique

The following examples detail the use of lighting that was done for my stop-motion short *No Exit?* (C-Clamp Pictures, 1998). The film takes place inside a castle dungeon during a dark and stormy evening, and chronicles a skeleton's ill-fated attempts at escaping from this prison.

Figure 3-18 shows the establishing shot, which "establishes" the location of the story and the overall mood. Skeletons of deceased prisoners hang shackled on the wall, or are stretched out on racks, hanging in a stockade, or tortured with some other device. To heighten this depressed mood, the cinematographer, Lance O. Soltys, decided that the mood would be best augmented if we bathed the set with a blue light.

There are several key lights in Figure 3-18: one lights the skeletons in the sarcophagus and on the rack

Figure 3-18

and the wall behind it, another lights the skeleton in the hanging cage, and a third lights the skeleton to the right, in the stocks. A fill light (with a blue filter in front of it) is bathing the entire set to create the emotion.

Figure 3-19 is the doorway into the dungeon (seen from inside the dungeon). The effect wanted here was one of contrast. The walls of the dungeon

Figure 3-19

are still bathed in blue, but just beyond the door is a reddish-orange flickering light to simulate and off-camera torch. Since the main character in the story (a skeleton brought to life) wishes to escape from the dungeon, the point here was to make the other side

of the door desirable. Our eyes tend to gravitate toward lighter colors, and so the doorway becomes the center of attention for the skeleton.

To bring the skeleton to life, a bolt of lightning from a raging thunderstorm enters the room through a window. To set up the effect, a light was placed just outside the window and turned on for a couple of frames. This created the initial flash of the bolt (Fig. 3-20A).

Figure 3-20A

As the bolt enters the room, there is a great flash of light (Fig. 3-20B). This establishes the initial light as it bathes the room. The effect was achieved by overexposing the scene with two to three frames.

Figure 3-20B

Finally, the lightning bolt itself enters and strikes the skeleton (Fig. 3-20C). The spotlight outside the window was left on during the duration of the lightning strike (about 72 frames, or 3 seconds)

Figure 3-20C

more on the blue side, thus continuing with the feeling of "coldness" inside the damp dungeon. The niche inside the wall that the skeleton has just emerged from is left dark so that the whiteness of the bones can stand out more. When designing your shots, make sure that you do not overdesign your background, or the audience will not concentrate on the object(s) in the scene that you want them to.

Figure 3-21

to help sell the idea that the bolt is coming from outside. This effect was created by first filming the scene for 72 frames, adding yet another light behind the skeleton inside the wall niche (lower right-hand corner of the frame) allowed for interactive lighting on the skeleton itself as it is being struck. The shutter was then closed on the camera and backwound 72 frames to the beginning of the shot. An easel with an animation peg board was placed between the camera and miniature set and the shutter reopened. Black velvet was then hung on the easel and the animation of the bolt was created by painting white poster paint on 72 animation cels. Care had to be taken to ensure that the bolt went behind the chain that is suspending the hanging cage. To further sell the effect, shards of lightning particles were animated bouncing off the skeleton as the lightning strikes it. Each cel was photographed and thus "burned" into the negative as a multiple exposure. Since lightning has a somewhat nebulous edge, the shutter was closed again and the film backwound 72 frames once more. The animation cels we rephotographed, but this time the lens was taken slightly out of focus. When the film was finally processed and projected, an illusion was created of a lightning bolt coming through the window and striking a skeleton, complete with interactive lightning.

Figure 3-21 is a shot of the skeleton, recently brought to life, looking about the room as it nonchalantly scratches its arm. The light continues to be

Later in the film, the skeleton has walked over to the staircase leading up to the doorway (Fig. 3-22). As it begins to ascend the stairs, we can see interactive lighting of its front that is coming from the torch on the other side of the door.

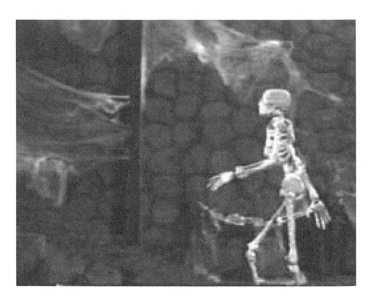

Figure 3-22

By the time the skeleton has reached to top of the stairs, we are afforded three contrasting colors: the reddish-orange hue of the off-screen torch, the cold dark blue of the walls of the dungeon, and finally the white of the skeleton's bones (our primary point of interest), which stands out from the blue of the walls (Fig. 3-23).

Now that we have a basic understanding of lighting, let us move on to performance and acting as it applies to the animated medium.

Figure 3-23

CHAPTER 4

Fundamentals of Animation Acting

Animation performance uses the following to convey thought and action:

Key poses (the foundation of performance, or interpretation of a character)

1. Anticipation
2. **In-between**
3. Ease-in
4. Ease-out
5. Follow-through
6. **Overlapping action**
7. **Holds** (pausing)
8. **Squash and stretch** (this is common in cel animation, rare in stop-motion, and can be mimed, to a very limited extent, in live-action)

These are the building blocks of successful motion, and since performance is comprised of motion, they must become the foundation of your animation acting.

The Key Pose

When a live actor performs on stage or screen, his movements are a combination of very subtle and overt primary gestures or poses (bodily and facial), followed by ancillary poses that fill in the primaries. If you filmed an actor going through his action, and then developed the film and analyzed the performance frame by frame, you would will discover key poses.

All movement can be broken down into primary poses that lay the foundation of the entire action. These primary poses (keys) give emotional content to the action, and are filled in by secondary poses, or in-betweens, to smooth out the action. This principle, the foundation of animation for decades, is seen in real-life motion. Key poses are the "thought" of the performance. Key poses describe the emotion and dynamic action of the character, and without them, the performance is dull, ambiguous, and without a specific goal.

Mr. Rat

Fine art sculptors do a great deal of thinking about how they are going to sculpt their figures. Indeed, the best way to study pose is to simply look to the masters of sculpture, such as Michelangelo, Auguste Rodin, and Frederick Remington. Well thought-out sculpture has form, metaphor, pose, weight, and movement.

Therefore, one might think of a key pose as an individual sculpture that can exist on its own and provide a story or thought through its shape alone.

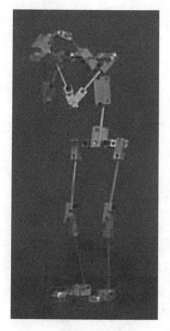

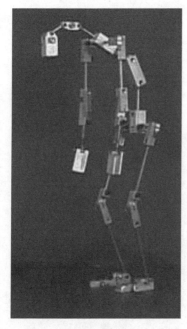

Figure 4-1   Figure 4-2

Through simple pose, one can impart a tremdous range of emotions. Figure 4-1 might suggest emotional pain.

Figure 4-2 may imply exhaustion.

And Figure 4-3 might imply shyness.

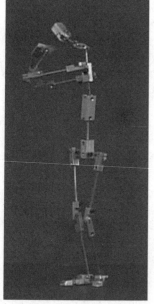

Figure 4-3

characters via the key pose. After that, these keys would be passed on to an assistant called the in-betweener, whose job it was to fill in the poses *between* the keys, and thus flesh out the motion. The key and in-between drawings were then passed on to the ink and paint department, and finally off to the cameraman for the final shoot. This process has lasted to the present day when producing cel-animated films. When it comes to stop-motion animation, however, the in-betweener does not exist, and here's why.

STRAIGHT-AHEAD LINEAR ANIMATION

In traditional cel animation, the drawings of the key poses as well as the in-betweens exist on paper, and as such, can be referenced back to if there is a problem. If the animation director wishes to change or slightly modify a drawing, all he needs to do is refer to the drawing in question and correct or re-place it with another. In short, the drawings are tangible and readily accessible. Stop-motion animation does not afford this luxury.

The stop-motion puppet is a tangible, three-dimensional object that exists in the real world, enabling the actor/animator to walk up to the model and position it during single-frame animation in three-dimensional space. It is an exclusively straight-ahead form of animation (sometimes called "through" animation). The stop-motion puppet is in-variably a single object, and not a series of objects (with the exception of **replacement animation**). And because it is a single object, it must be posed during single-frame photography to create a sense of motion. It is *linear* animation, as one must go from point A to point B before the shot is completed.

One might think of cel animation as a form of nonlinear animation, allowing the animator to skip back and forth in his animation drawings to correct, fudge, and alter keys and in-between drawings, even inserting additional in-betweens or keys if he wishes. And since cels can be referred back to, employing an in-betweener is quite simple to do. An assistant can produce the in-between poses while the key animator can move on to the next scene. Imagine, however, a key animator posing a stop-motion puppet into a key

The In-Between, as Applied to Stop-Motion Animation

As animation began to evolve in the first half of the 20th century, it found its primary roots in cel (hand-drawn) animation. Early proponents of this art form, such as Walt Disney and the Fleischer Brothers, found that audiences enjoyed this new art and wanted more. When it became evident that the process could be streamlined into a sort of "assembly-line" method, the studios hired expert draftsmen (who also had acting sensibilities) to plan and draw out the primary action of the animated pose, then stepping away while an assistant positions the puppet through its in-between paces until just one frame before the key pose. The assistant steps away from the table and lets the key animator step back in and pose the puppet into its next key pose. This would, at best, be a rather senseless and time-wasting method of animating in stop-motion. Stop-motion works best when a single animator creates the key poses as well as the in-betweens during the linear animation process.

Indeed, once the puppet has been moved to its next position, the position where it was at *previously* is lost forever and cannot be altered on a frame-by-frame basis once the animation has been shot. Even with **surface gauges** and modern-day frame-grabbing capabilities (such as video-assist equipment for storing and capturing frames for playback), these devices do not solve the problem of being able to easily refer back to specific frames even after the animation has been shot, and insert, edit, replace, or modify a single pose as one can in cel or **cgi** animation.

While not impossible, it is extremely difficult, if not maddening, to go back to a frame of a stop-motion sequence, remove it, then try one's best to match the in-between successfully between two keys and retake the frame. The equipment must allow for the insertion of a frame, and none that are broadcast quality presently do. Cel animation is two-dimensional (height and width, with a simulated depth via perspective). Stop-motion is uniquely three-dimensional during the shooting of the animation, and exists in three planes (height, width, and depth) on the animation tabletop. Since the animator must position the model in frame sequence from point A to point B, he/she is required to pose the model not only in its key poses, but must fill in the in-betweens while he/she progresses toward the completion of the shot, hitting the keys when necessary. In other words, he/she cannot pose the puppet into key pose number 14 until he/she has posed and shot the last in-between coming out of key pose number 13. This can be an especially disconcerting way to animate for someone not accustomed to animating both the keys and the in-betweens at once.

Anticipation

The physics of movement are very complex, and while it is not necessary for an actor to receive a PhD in physics to understand movement, we humans have seen things move throughout our lives, and we intuitively expect organic and mechanical bodies to behave in certain ways, based upon our years of experience observing things moving in the world. When an animated character has a wrong move applied to it, it will look odd and may not be believable. Often, it is best to simply observe and study the movement of all types of things (animals, humans, insects, even machines) to get the best reference material.

There is an old physics saying that goes, "*For every action, there is an opposite and equal reaction.*" Anticipation is somewhat like this. A classic example of anticipation is in the process of kicking something, say, a soccer ball. If a character is standing in front of a soccer ball and suddenly throws his leg out toward the ball and kicks it, it would look unnatural because there was no "wind-up" leading into the kick, which is what happens in real life.

Instead, the character cocks his leg backward, there is a slight pause (anticipating the kick) as the character studies the object to be kicked, and then he throws his leg forward violently and kicks the ball (Figs. 4-4, 4-5, 4-6). This wind-up is the anticipation.

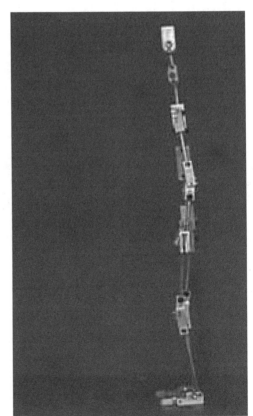

Figure 4-4

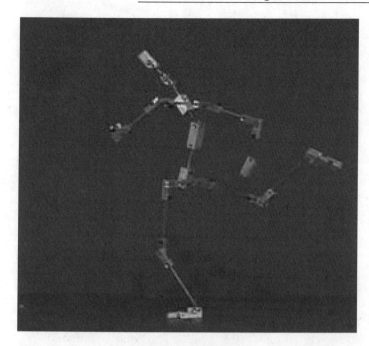

Figure 4-5

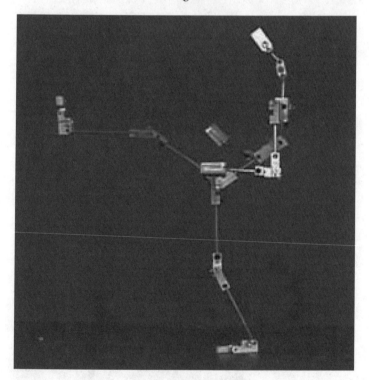

Figure 4-6

position and gradually accelerates to a point where a consistent speed is maintained. Then, once the motion is winding down, the speed decelerates to a stop. For example, if an automobile needs to accelerate from zero to 90 miles per hour, it is impossible for it to go from a dead stop to 90 miles per hour in an instant. No automobile can do this. Rather, the vehicle must gradually work its way up to 90 miles per hour by accelerating. Ease-out refers to the object gradually accelerating, while ease-in implies a gradual slowing down of the object. Even a bullet traveling from a gun will have ease-in and ease-out, though it happens so fast that it is inconsequential to the naked eye. The trigger hammer strikes the surface of the bullet. This ignites the gunpowder, and the bullet disengages from the shell casing and travels the length of the gun barrel and out into the world toward its target. If the bullet does not hit anything, it gradually slows down until gravity forces it to drop to the ground.

In the case of an arm swinging forward, ease-out would be used to gradually accelerate the arm (Figs. 4-7, 4-8, 4-9, 4-10).

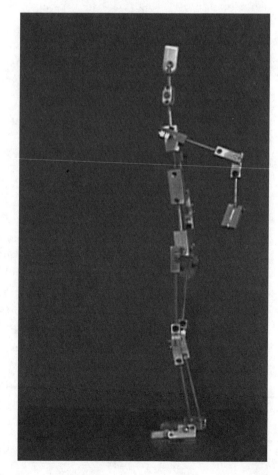

Ease-In and Ease-Out

Sometimes referred to as slow-in and slow-out, this process deals with the idea that all movement (regardless of how fast or slow it is) goes from a resting

Figure 4-7

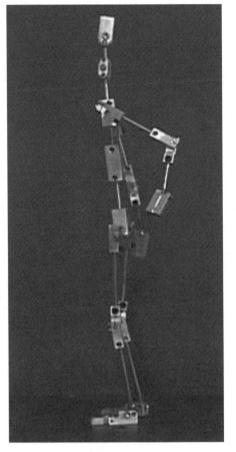

Figure 4-8

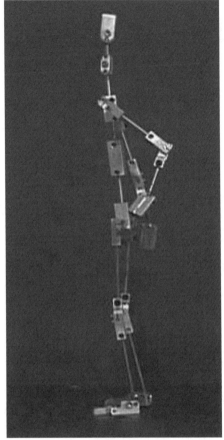

Figure 4-9

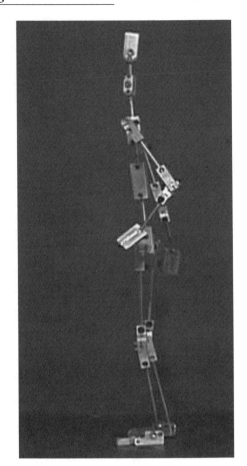

Figure 4-10

The next two positions would be the in-betweens (Figs. 4-11, 4-12).

To gradually slow the arm to a stop, **ease-in** would be needed (Figs. 4-13, 4-14, 4-15, 4-16).

Most other types of objects (save for light waves and Mr. Anderson in *The Matrix*, 1999) do not travel bullet time and can be gauged using ease-in and ease-out during the animation process. Once the stop-motion subject being animated has ease-in and ease-out applied to its movement (and provided that the in-between positions are consistent, one to the next), the animation begins to take on a very naturalistic and smooth appearance.

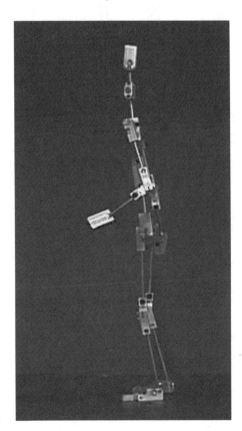

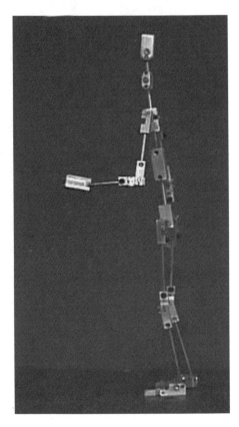

Figures 4-11 and 4-12

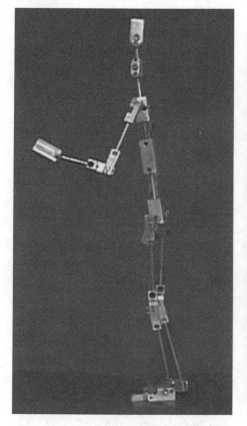

Figure 4-13

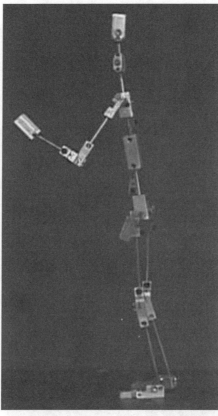

Figure 4-14

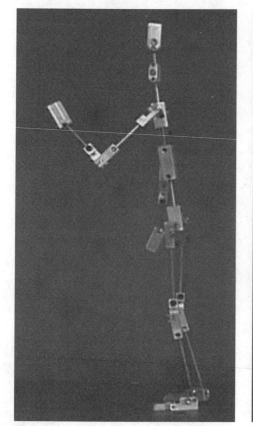

Figure 4-15

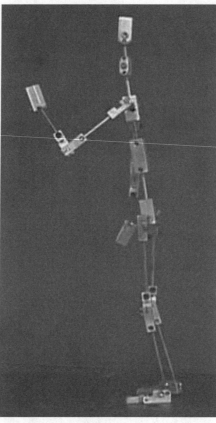

Figure 4-16

Smoothness, however, does not guarantee a performance. In fact, it is a truism that smooth animation does not necessarily make great performance animation, though the **strobe** effect and occasional "popping" of the animation is forgiving if the performance is there. This is an odd paradox, but one that is very important to remember. To illustrate, in his Academy Award nominated stop-motion short *Next* (1989) filmmaker and animator Barry Purves brings William Shakespeare onstage to audition for a play. In the course of three and a half minutes, Shakespeare offers an acting tour de force in which he acts a brief sequence from nearly every play he has ever written. The animation in this film, while not necessarily *technically* smooth, is absolutely exceptional in its use of performance. The audience knows *exactly* what the character is doing and feeling, and the key poses help to make next a magnificent feast for the eye.

Follow-Through

To some extent, **follow-through** might be thought of as the opposite of anticipation. Whereas the latter deals with action occurring before the main action, follow-through keeps the action going once the primary action is finished. For example, as a discus thrower goes into his windup (anticipation), he then flings his arm and body forward and lets the discus fly. As the discus leaves his hand and goes on its journey, the thrower's arm still continues around the body, eventually coming to rest. Such latter ancillary action after the main action allows the arm to continue (follow-through) and complete the action. In the case of an automobile wreck, a speeding car hits a brick wall and stops violently. If the driver is not wearing his seatbelt, the inertia of the speeding car suddenly coming to a halt propels the driver into the dashboard or through the windshield. The car has stopped, but the driver's follow-through action continues until either his own power or an obstructing object stops him.

Overlapping Action

If one takes the time to observe humans and animals walking and moving about, much of the action that they do is based on action that overlaps each other. Overlapping action is based on the premise that the appendages of most bodies do not move at the same time; in fact, they are almost invariably staggered. If someone moved his/her arms up over his/her heads, so that both arms moved at the same speed and symmetry, and did this continually throughout his/her life, the action would get profoundly boring. Rather, it is generally best to stagger the movements by offsetting the **timing** of individual appendages. If a character has to push on a locked door with both arms, have one arm rise up before the other arm does. Overlapping this action makes the movements appear more natural and true to life.

Holds

Without holds (or pauses) in everyday gestures and movement, life would get monotonous. The simple paradox is that movement is replete with pauses. However, stop-motion animation works best when puppets are moving in such a way that, even when they appear to be resting, they appear to be moving somewhat. There are many (albeit brief) holds in cel animation, as this type of animation is more forgiving when the movement pauses momentarily. However, since stop-motion puppets are actual three-dimensional objects, the audience expects them to be moving on a continual basis, because that is how we perceive real-life objects in everyday situations. The

moment a puppet ceases movement and freezes, it appears unnatural, or at the very least crosses over into the realm of the cartoon. This isn't bad, but if one is attempting the more realistic movements of everyday life, freezing the movements totally on puppets will detract from this realism.

To illustrate, say, one is animating a character walking up to a refrigerator and opening the door. Once the door is opened, the puppet looks at the contents of the fridge. A less experience animator may just freeze the puppet in front of the fridge as it looks inside. A better solution would be to give the action a bit more life by moving the arms slightly while the puppet is resting, or perhaps moving the head side to side as the character inspects the contents of the fridge. In short, keep the action going in some way or another, no matter how subtle the movement. This greatly aids the performance.

Squash and Stretch

Traditionally, cel animation has used the principles of squash and stretch to give bounce and vitality to animated characters. The clay medium is especially appropriate to squash and stretch due to its extreme pliability (Figs. 4-17, 4-18, 4-19).

Squash and stretch, therefore, has a rather singu-

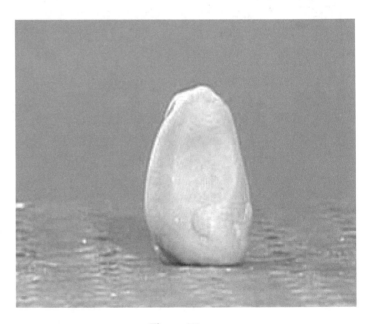

Figure 17

Figure 4-18

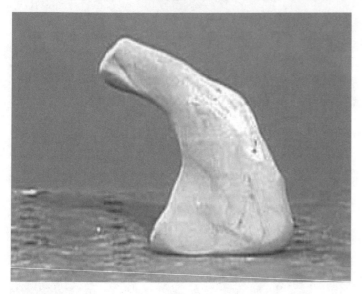

Figure 4-19

down. And certainly in the area of clay animation, the pliability of clay allows an infinite way to manipulate one's character.

ARCS AND TRAJECTORIES

All movement has **arcs** and trajectories. An arm rising upward follows an arc, and an arrow that is shot from a bow follows a linear **trajectory** to its target (Figs. 4-20A and 4-20B).

Arcs and trajectories are not terribly difficult to do in cel or computer-generated animation, because arcs and trajectories can be planned on paper or drawn out in advance on a piece of clear acetate that is hung over a computer screen.

In the case of stop-motion, however, the process becomes more complex because the animator is manipulating the puppet in three-dimensional space, in a frame-by-frame process. The object (arm, leg, pigtail, etc.) must remain on these imaginary arcs or trajectory lines in the three-dimensional space at all times and this can be quite difficult if one loses ones concentration or isn't paying attention. If the puppet comes off these lines, a stutter or "pop" effect will occur once the animation is played back, resulting in

larly "animatey" or cartoon look and feel to it that is peculiar to hand-drawn cel animation. Squash and stretch can be accomplished in stop-motion by using clay characters to very good effect. However, this obviously imparts a "cartoony" look to the animation, which is fine if one is going for that appearance. One very successful sequence using squash and stretch in stop-motion puppetry is the Yawning Man sequence from the George Pal fantasy film *Tom Thumb* (1958). To achieve the effect of the puppet stretching up and squashing down, animator Gene Warren utilized a threaded dowel rod which allowed him to turn incrementally for single-frame animation. As the rod would turn, it would either push the puppet up or bring it

Figure 4-20A

Figure 4-20B

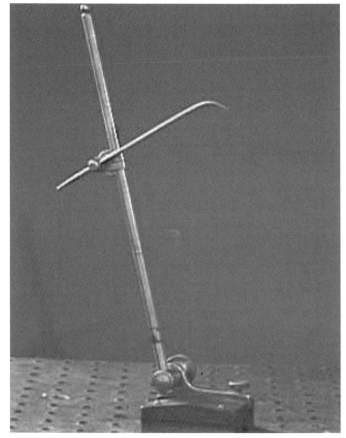

Figure 4-21

a visual distraction. If it happens a lot, the animation will be very difficult to watch and the audience may find it annoying.

There are a few techniques that stop-motion animators have used over the years to maintain consistency of arc/trajectory movement in three-dimensional space during single-frame manipulation. The traditional way is the use of the venerable surface gauge (Fig. 4-21).

A tool used in the industrial trades, stop-motion animators have used the surface gauge for decades. It serves a threefold purpose:

1. It measures how far one has moved a puppet in space.
2. The scriber shows where the puppet was at after it has been moved.
3. It helps the animator by keeping the puppet on its arc/trajectory at all times.

The gauge is comprised of a base, knob adjustor, spindle, rod, and scriber, and is especially useful if the puppet has to walk or run. In the case of a walk, the puppet is tied down on the animation tabletop

and the gauge is placed behind the puppet, with the scriber pointing and almost touching the back of the puppet (Fig. 4-22).

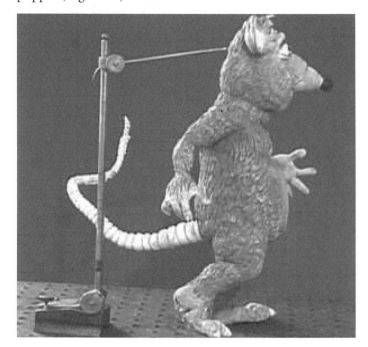

Figure 4-22

The scriber's pointed end is marked at a spot on the puppet that the animator uses each time he moves the puppet (the mark could be a particular scale, wart, skin wrinkle, the head of a small pushpin, or even a piece of tape, as long as the tape or pin cannot be seen by the camera.

As the puppet is pushed forward, the space where it was previously is lost, but since the gauge has not been moved, the scriber's pointed end tells the animator where the puppet was previously (Fig. 4-23).

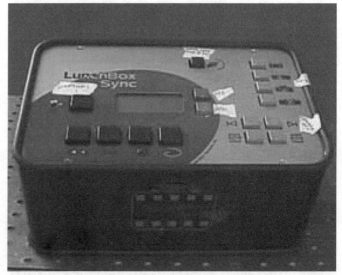

Figure 4-24

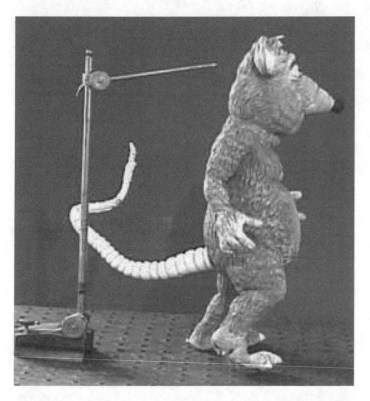

Figure 4-23

In this way, the animator can gauge how far the puppet has been moved, which is critical information when measuring in-between increments. And as long as the scriber's pointed end is place at the mark for each succeeding frame, the movement of the puppet will remain in a constant trajectory as it walks forward, because the animator is gauging the model in the same place for every frame.

Another, albeit more recent, tool used by stop-motion animators for gauging puppet movement is the use of a frame grabber, or a simple video camera and TV monitor screen (Fig. 4-24).

Before the advent of video grabbing, filmmakers had to shoot their work and send the footage off to the lab for processing. They had to then wait a day or two before the processed film could be viewed. Now that we are living in the video and digital era, one can shoot animation and review it instantly by using video/digital assist technology.

The frame grabber is either an analog or digital capture system that enables the animator to store frames for instant playback and/or for assistance in registering animation one frame at a time (one might think of this as an electronic surface gauge). If the device is analog, the camera is connected to the capture device via RCA cables, and this in turn is connected to a TV monitor. Once the animation has been shot, the animator can play back the animation off the device and see it on the TV monitor. The most common and frequently used system currently on the market is the Video Lunchbox manufactured by Animation Toolworks in Portland, Oregon. This device can be used for either stop-motion or cel animation, making it ideal for quick motion testing.

If the device is digital, then the camera is plugged into the computer either by Firewire or USB connection (depending on the manufacturer). The software is opened up on the computer, and the animator can then see the animation played back on any proprietary digital monitors that the software has. The DSP Perception Player is a common digital frame-grabbing device. As long as one has a video capture card, Adobe Premiere's stop-motion capability can be used to capture frames. Once the animation has been captured, it can be saved as a movie file (such as .mov or .avi).

The Work of the Timing Director

Once the performance has been settled upon, the actor must then translate this action to the animated character. Since the character exists only as a lifeless stop-motion puppet, the actor is then faced with the daunting task of breaking this movement down in sections (blocks) as he puts the puppet through its paces frame by frame, breathing life into the puppet. In non-dialogue scenes, there is certainly room for improvisation (especially in a time-lapse process like animation, where the actor can often obtain inspiration to move the puppet in a way he had not thought about earlier. However, thinking about the performance and action *before* animating is crucial, because it will aid the actor in the timing of the action in question. In addition, any improvisation must generally be relegated to the secondary action of the performance. This improvisation is generally found in a hand gesture, eye blinking, or something comparable that doesn't take a lot of time to do, but yet stays within the required time frame of the blocked scene.

BLOCKING THE SCENE

The term **blocking** is borrowed from theater. A stage director looks at the script, confers with the actors as to the interpretation of the character (how they behave, who they are, etc.) and then directs the actor or actors through the scene by telling them when and where to move, and where to stop as they say their lines. Some film or stage directors exact considerable control as to how actors interpret a character's personality, while others prefer to simply block the action and let the actors interpret the personality. The latter director is probably the more prudent. Because actors spend their lives learning how to interpret personality for the character they are portraying, they can bring a great deal of depth, introspection, revelation, and emotion to the character. The director should take advantage of this. While actors must follow the spoken dialogue of the play, they will let their instincts drive their character to behave in a certain way by creating interpretation.

The timing director (TD) must break the scene down into its basic action elements, so that the animator knows where the characters must go and what they need to do to get there.

Two different conductors of Beethoven's Fifth Symphony will invariably interpret the composer's music differently. The notes are still the same on the printed score, but timing and **spacing** of the music will not be the same, because one conductor may interpret certain passages as being slower, may pause more in silence, or balance the instruments differently than the other conductor would. The two performances may sound the same because they are using the same score (script), but they are not.

For example, consider the following dialogue that your animated character might need to say to his friend:

"Will you come here?"

The actor can place an emphasis on any one of those words, but the meaning will be different.

"**Will** you come here?" infers that the character is asking his friend if he would consider coming here, but depending on posture, it can also suggest that the character is *demanding* his friend to come here.

"Will **you** come here?" implies that if there is more than one character being addressed, "you" can mean a specific person. The character may even point defiantly at the friend (a teacher pointing to a recalcitrant eight-year-old student, for example).

"Will you **come** here?"

This may suggest movement, as opposed to "Will you **stay** here?"

"Will you come **here**?" could mean that the friend must come here, not over there.

This is how an actor might interpret the spoken line. If the character stomps his foot when he says *"**Will** you come here?"* his friend knows that the character is not offering a request. He means business and might be angry.

IMAGE	Frame	ACTION	ACTION	ACTION	ACTION
MOUTH "O"	1	RAISES ARM			
	2			STOMPS FOOT	
	3				
	4				
	5	LOOKS LEFT			
	6				
	7				
MOUTH "V"	8				
	9				
	10				
MOUTH "E"	12				
	13				
	14				
	15				
	16				
MOUTH R	17				
	18				
	19				
	20				
	21				
	22				
	23				
	24				

Figure 4-25

Actual behavior (secondary action) that motivates the character to do certain things while moving through the directed environment is up to the actor. Blocking is the blueprint of the action within a scene governed by the director, and performance is born out of the actor's interpretation (usually with the assistance of the director) of how his character behaves during his journey through the blocked environment. In a time-lapse process like animation, it is generally imperative that a scene be blocked out to the nth degree, because it will take many days, if not weeks, to shoot a particular scene. In addition, animators must know when and where the character says a bit of dialogue as he moves through the environment. And the only real way to do this is to create exposure sheets of the dialogue (Fig. 4-25).

There are many types of exposures sheets, but they all have a couple of things in common. There is a column for making notes as to what vowel, consonant, or extreme expression the animator is to use on the puppet, and another column that marks individual frames. There can be additional columns to allow the animator to write notes as to the action. In Figure 4-25, the left-most column allows one to write in the mouth or face expression. As indicated, the vowel "O" is to last from frame 1 through frame 7, the consonant "V" is to last 8 through 10, and so on. Looking to the columns on the right, one can write notes that tell the animator what the character needs to do action-wise: frames 1 through 4 he raises his arm, and frames 2 through 7 he stomps his foot. This is an example of using exposure sheets to create overlapping action.

However, before one can create the exposure sheet, one must, of course, analyze the soundtrack. Traditionally, this has been done using magnetic stock and read with a sequencer or flatbed editing bench (such as a Steenbeck). However, digital technology has made this process easier. By creating a .wav file of one's dialogue track, the .wav can then be imported into a sound-editing software such as Magpie Pro(tm), Adobe Premiere, or Sound Edit 16. The software then enables the animator to break down the individual syllables of the words frame by frame. This information can then be transferred to the exposure sheets.

TIMING AND SPACING

Someone might ask: How many frames does it take Mother Hubbard to get to the cupboard and pull out a bone for her dog? The answer: It depends. Timing and pacing of movement is contingent on what is happening in the scene and the extenuating circumstances within the scene. If Mother Hubbard has arthritis in her hips, it's going to take her a while to get to the cupboard, certainly longer than if she didn't have arthritis. Or maybe she's healthy and can run a mile in 10 minutes, but can't remember which cupboard she put the bone in. She idly stands there, trying to make a decision as to which cupboard door the bone is behind. Meanwhile, her impatient dog is tapping his foot.

How many frames does it take for a character to raise his arm to wave at somebody? The answer: It depends on how the character feels at that moment and how motivated he is to raise his arm. Solution: Look at the script and ask the director, then create an interpretation of that scene based on your skill as an actor.

In short, how many frames does anything take? The answer: It depends. This is why acting anything out with one's body and/or mental acumen is vital to the interpretation of the timing of the performance. Just as no two actors will interpret a scene in exactly the same way, so too, no two actors or animators will interpret a scene the same way. That is what makes any performance original.

One of the difficulties in any type of animation is making sure that the animation lasts long enough on the screen so that the audience can gather the information and interpret it the way the actor/animator wants it to be interpreted. All too often, budding animators tend to animate an action too fast, preventing the audience from taking the time necessary to absorb and interpret the action. Timing and pose are critical for a proper interpretation. The timing of a slow, lumbering walk of an elephant must obviously last longer than the quick, fleeting arboreal hops of a spider monkey from one branch to another. Spacing, therefore, is contingent on the timing of the action. Once the timing has been worked out, one must then plan out the action by spacing the keys and in-betweens accordingly. One of the best ways to learn the process of timing and spacing is to acquire real footage of what is being animated. For example, if one is animating a spider monkey jumping from one branch to another, try to obtain a DVD or video of these creatures in the wild performing such maneuvers. If you live near a zoo, take a video camera and film them. Later, you can analyze the footage for timing and spacing purposes. Remember, the best source of research is the real McCoy.

In Figure 4-26, we have the classic bouncing ball example. Notice how as the ball falls, the positions are close together (this is the **ease-out**). As it falls,

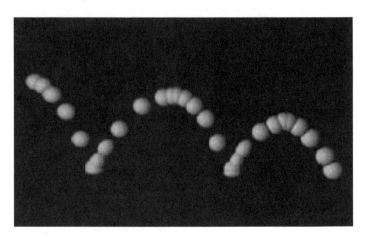

Figure 4-26

the ball accelerates, impacting the ground and squishing. As it bounces up again, it eases out, easing in again toward the top of the second bounce as gravity takes hold to slow down its bounce. It eases out again as it proceeds to fall again, and so on.

An object that is dropped will move at varying speeds depending on how high it was dropped. In this instance, the ball has been dropped from a height of a few feet, and therefore has not had sufficient *time* to accelerate at a great deal of speed prior to hitting the ground. The height of the drop will hence determine the timing of the bounce, as well as the spacing. If the ball is dropped from the top of the St. Louis Gateway Arch (620 feet), the ball will then have more time gaining speed. Once it hits the ground, the considerable speed it has acquired through the fall will allow for a much more forceful impact once it hits the ground, and the ball will bounce higher.

Acting

While the following statement might be an overgeneralization, it could be said that acting is *the art of creating a performance in which an actor pretends to be someone else or some thing, for a certain amount of time, that the actor is (generally) not in real life.* It is an illusion. It takes a great deal of training, concentration, experience, and imagination to successfully convince an audience that you are what you appear to be (i.e., someone else) for one and a half to two hours. Acting is a reflection of the human condition told in story, and attempts to explain why we are the way we are, how we got that way, where we were and are in life, where we are going, and our interaction with other characters while at the same time conveying all of this to the audience.

Animators may be creating the illusion of life artificially, but is it not life? Actors create an illusion of the life of a character. So do they differ all that much? Let's discuss this concept for a moment.

As stated before, actors are illusionists. Their job is to create a character. Regardless of whether it is stage, radio, or film acting, there is a tremendous amount of concentration that is involved in keeping and sustaining the illusion of a character. Each process has its own set of challenges, problems, and solutions. In a theatrical play, the continuity is ongoing and a rhythm is sustained, but at the price of keeping it going for one to two hours, it can be exhausting for the actor(s), physically as well as emotionally. In film work, the script is almost invariably shot out of sequence to save time and money. If Scene Five takes place in Joe's bar, and Scene 18 is also in Joe's bar, why not shoot both scenes on the same day while the cast and crew are at the Joe's bar set? Narrative filmmaking is therefore a nonlinear process. Since filmmaking is a time-lapse process drawn out anywhere from a few days to 12 weeks, an actor performing in a film must know precisely the level of emotion of his character for any given scene. Matching the level of emotion for a scene that is shot over a period of several days or weeks is, at best, a rather daunting task. Once the shots are edited together and run in a theater, the actor's level of intensity must match from shot to shot or the audience might pick up on it. This process is no different for the animation actor.

WHY ACT?

Most actors enjoy make-believe and being someone else, as it gives them a uniquely creative way to learn about and express human behavior. I don't think actors ever really grow up, or at least they remember what it was like to be a child. As children, we all role-played because it was fun. When we grow up, most of us lose that sense of play and fall into the responsibilities of adulthood and the nine-to-fiver. There are a select few who somehow retain this roleplaying and channel it into a career as an actor.

As of this writing, the art of film acting is roughly a hundred years old, and animation is at least that. Stage acting is centuries old. On stage, the actor in the **proscenium** must play to the back of the house, so that the entire audience can see the performance (depending, of course, on the size of the theater house). Performance in early silent cinema (indeed in early talkies as well), however, is wrought with "stagey" performance, because the actor was struggling with the new medium of cinema and applying stage acting principles of broad body and facial gestures to the cinematic screen when it wasn't necessary. It took a few decades before it became obvious that the film screen is quite large, and that the actor's face could be in the lap of the audience with the use of a close-up. Pulling back on the performance was, therefore, a necessity.

As animation evolved through the 20th century, it became specific to hand-drawn artwork. Concurrent with animated art was the animated puppet film, and in just the past 12 years, commercial feature film computer animation. Much animation in the history of film is wrapped up in the cel-animated cartoon, with comical situations, slapstick, and absurdist reality in which objects appear from nowhere, characters explode, fall apart, squash and stretch, and change shape, miraculously coming back together in the next shot. As such, most of humanity who has seen animation regards it as funny and absurdist, and hence, synonymous with comedy and satire. However, it need not be, and can take advantage of serious drama as well.

COMPARISON OF LIVE ACTION AND ANIMATION PERFORMANCE

I would like to offer two statements about the art of acting and animation:

1. *Acting is the creative art of imbuing oneself with a role one is to assay.*
2. *Character animation is the creative art of imbuing an animated subject (cel, stop-motion, marionettes, computer-generated, etc.) with a role it is to assay.*

Well, that's a mouthful.

If both of these statements are true (and I believe they are), then allow me to be bold enough to combine both statements and rephrase it thus:

Acting is the interpretive art of an actor creating a role that finds its outlet through the stage, radio, or screen, using himself and possibly a secondary (i.e., animation or real-time puppetry) surrogate character to act through, to create a performance in an attempt to explore the human condition for an audience.

Over the years, I have found myself closing the

gap on live acting and acting through the medium of animation in large part because they seem to be working toward the same goal, namely, to perform via characterization. In fact, I have pretty much closed that gap. Therefore, in the remainder of this book, I will refer to the animator as actor, and refer to animation as technical process that an actor uses to create a performance.

REAL-TIME ACTING AND TIME-LAPSE ACTING

It is my opinion that there is little difference between live-action preparation for assaying a role and an animator's assaying a role for a character that he is creating. Both are creating characters that will come to life, have breath, and hopefully impart realness to the audience, as is the actor's craft. There is, however, one fundamental difference, and it is this:

1. Actors perform in real time.
2. Animators perform in real time *and time lapse.*

The actor of stage and screen uses his own body and voice (unless the part is mimed) to create the character, acting the role out in real time and space.

The actor using the animation process uses his body and mind's eye to block out the performance in real time and space. However, once the movement is rehearsed, the actor/animator must then translate this performance into a time-lapse process by applying it to the character to be animated, *one frame at a time.* This necessitates the actor breaking down the action into blocks and then timing these blocks so that they will come together as a seamless whole. When 24 frames have been shot, one second of action has taken place. For the actor using animation, the difficulty comes in trying to wed the technical aspects of these blocks and yet retain the aesthetic essence of the performance. With experience and training, this can be accomplished.

Real-time performance deals with the process whereby an audience views the performance of the actor at the same moment that the actor is assaying it. This is especially true for the stage. For a motion-picture performance, the actor has been recorded on film or digitally, and the audience experiences the performance in real time (i.e., 24 frames per second [film] or 30 samples per second [digital]). The actor is not actually there at the same time as the audience experiences the performance, but the audience experiences it nonetheless via the recorded medium, at the same speed and for the same duration as the actor originally interpreted it.

When an actor uses the animation medium to create a performance, he will sometimes use his own body in the studio to act out the character, or he will use his mind's eye (imagination) to mentally "see" the character going through its motion. This is real-time performance. The action is happening in the moment of the actor interpreting the performance for his own benefit.

Time-lapse occurs the moment when the actor begins to apply these timed-out blocks to frame-by-frame sequencing. The actor is no longer working in real time, but must now translate the action by moving the puppet in space, stepping out of the shot, clicking the frame, stepping back into the shot and moving the puppet again.

GET INTO THE CHARACTER'S MIND: EMOTION AND EXPRESSION

Finally, action by itself is not enough. One must be able to feel and impart the emotional content of the action in question, as well as proper facial expression. While emotion and action go hand in hand to create the performance, emotion plays a tremendous part in getting the audience involved with your character. Emotion can be very obvious or it can be very, very subtle. It is emotion that any actor (stage, screen, radio, or animation) must tap into if he is to sell the performance to an audience. Here is an illustration of what I am talking about. If a female character has just found out that her spouse has just died in a car accident, she may throw her head back and scream, then fall to the floor in a huge gesture of dramatic overplay, and the audience may offer up thunderous applause for such a dramatic performance. But say you have the same scenario, only this time when the woman finds out her husband has died, she quietly sits down and her child comes up to her. A

solitary tear falls down the woman's cheek and her child touches it with his hand. The woman then embraces her child and they hold one another as if it were their last moment on earth. The audience weeps. Get the picture? An actor's job is to *get into the mind of the character* and make it believable. If the actor believes it (yes, even an animation actor), the audience just might, too, and for a moment, forget they are watching a play or film.

To illustrate this point further, there is a wonderful story of Disney animator Art Babbitt, who went to see a public showing of the 1941 film *Dumbo* (a film which he had worked on as one of the animation directors). During a sequence that was animated by animation legend William Tytla, Dumbo's mother is chained and locked up in a wagon cage of a circus. As Dumbo walks up to the door of the cage, his mother sticks out her trunk through the bars, recognizing Dumbo through her sense of touch. She then raises Dumbo in her truck and gently swings him back and forth, as if he were swinging in a baby carriage. Babbitt looked around and saw various women (probably mothers themselves) weeping. Babbitt realized that it was no longer animation, it was performance. A master actor (Tytla) had used the medium of animation to convey the power of emotion. What actor never attempts to convey the power of emotion? Never forget: We humans are *intensely* emotional creatures and are driven by it. When an audience forgets they are watching a play, film, or animation, and are caught up in your story and characters, they are hooked.

As mentioned earlier in this chapter, the key pose creates (or establishes) the thought of the action or motivation of a character. Without good key posing, communicating this thought and emotion to an audience is almost impossible. Successful acting and performance cannot be separated from pose, regardless of whether it is through real-time performance on stage or screen, or through time-lapse performance via the animation medium. Watch any competent actor on the stage or screen, and you will see this process happening. The actor assays the part he is interpreting by feeling the emotion of that character, and he uses his body to assist in conveying that emotion. Animators must be equally concerned about this conveyance. It must be noted, however, that there are many successful roads to interpreting a performance. For example, one actor may assay the role of Hamlet as a young man who is already insane, while another may interpret Hamlet as a young man who falls into insanity gradually. A third actor may interpret Hamlet as a young man who is not insane at all, but who is deeply angered and distraught over the death of his father and the subsequent injustices he feels have been perpetrated by his mother and uncle. Any of these interpretations may be justified. The point is that the actor has a responsibility to "find" the character, so that the audience is able to understand and follow along with the character during the story, based on what the actor feels was the intent of the playwright. It is therefore the responsibility of the animator to find the character he is working on as well.

For some people who are animators, this thought process might seem superfluous in its application to performance animation. Since I regard animation as a legitimate form of acting, I believe that any animator who is even remotely concerned about performance could (and should) learn from stage and screen actors. Indeed, animators should be encouraged to take acting classes themselves.

Since a comprehensive study of the art and craft of acting is beyond the scope of this manual, let us examine performance here as it applies to communicating emotion to an audience through body posture. Consider Figure 4-27.

Now take a look at Figure 4-28.

Apart from one another, these two poses can mean quite two different things. Note the upheld hand with the pointing finger and the clenched left hand of Figure 4-27, and the eyes appear mad or disdainful. We do not know the full story of this rat's predicament, but it looks as if he is angry or is having a political debate and is steadfastly refusing to budge on an issue. Conversely, Figure 4-28 can suggest indifference or apathy, or perhaps pensiveness (the drooped eyelids and arms to his sides). If these two shots were edited together (Figure 4-27 being the first shot, and then cutting to Figure 4-28), we would create a definite situation. The audience sees that Rat

Figure 4-27 (Rat 1)

Figure 4-28 (Rat 2)

1 is agitated about something and might be trying to make a point. When we cut to Rat 2, we see the source of his indignation, though Rat 2 seems indifferent or nonplussed about what Rat 1 is trying to get across. And it is this indifference that is agitating Rat 1.

Humans are continually reading the body posture of others. In fact, we do this for everything and not just humans, and we do it so often that it is something we take for granted. If we approach a tarantula in the wild and it lifts up its front legs and bares its fangs, we assume that it does not what to be bothered. A dog that rolls over on its back and exposes its stomach for a tummy rub is indicating through its body language that it trusts you to pet its tummy; meanwhile, you trust it that it won't bite you.

Let's create a key pose exercise. You are working on a feature film and the animation supervisor wants the rat to appear ashamed. So, in Figure 4-29 you pose the puppet in this fashion:

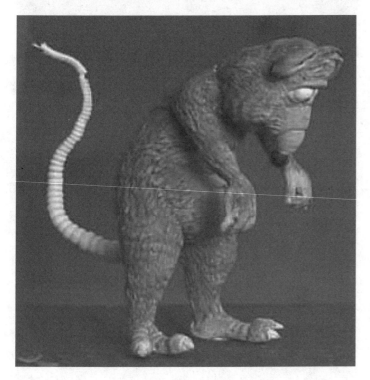

Figure 4-29

Let's talk about the key pose of Figure 4-29 for a moment. Does this reflect ashamedness? It may, but not very well. Let's examine why. Think of when you were a child and you did something wrong. If your parents found out about it, they would confront you

with the issue. If you realized that what you had done was wrong and admitted it, you would most likely have hung your head because you were ashamed of what you had done. OK, the rat is doing that. What else would you have done? You might have drooped your spine somewhat, as if you are ashamed to look up at your parents. Once again, the rat is doing that. Good. How would you have held your arms? Would you have placed your hands on your hips? Maybe, but probably not. That is more of a posture of defiance. Rather, you probably would have held your arms to your sides. In Figure 4-29, the rat has his arms down, but does it reflect the ashamedness of his posture? Not really. It looks more like he is getting ready to shoot some laser beams from his knuckles at an ant or grasshopper. And what about that tail? Since a rat has a tail, why not take full advantage of posing the tail in such a way that reflects being ashamed? Would it be rigid and standing up? It could, but it wouldn't accentuate being ashamed. Why not let it lie on the floor? Armed with these thoughts, let us re-pose the puppet to reflect these changes (Fig. 4-30).

Figure 4-30

Note now that in Figure 4-30 the arms and tail are completely limp. This begins to approach what we are after. However, it can also convey simply that he is looking at something on the ground. So, we've still not arrived at what we want. What other thing can we do to get the feeling of being ashamed? Take a look at Figure 4-31.

Figure 4-31

His head is turned to the audience and his eyes are closed, but now it looks like he is asleep. So that doesn't really work either. What can we do now? Let's open his eyes a bit and have him look at something O.S. (off-screen), and bring up an arm as well (Fig. 4-32).

Figure 4-32

This begins to approach something akin to being ashamed, but it can also imply being sly. Let's bring the other arm up, tilt his torso back so that he is slumped a bit, and tilt the head forward (Fig. 4-33).

Figure 4-33

Now we are beginning to get a posture toward being ashamed. In addition, the tail has been brought from outside his body space and into his body space (over the foot). His appendages are now contained within himself. Whenever we feel threatened or ashamed, we tend to physically retreat into our-selves, bringing our appendages closer together. We have just explored two fundamental aspects of the actor's art, body posture and gesture. Let's explore it again.

Once again, you are working on a feature film and the animation supervisor needs a shot where the rat is recoiling in fear as something O.S., after having been shoved to the ground. So you place the rat on the ground (Fig. 4-34).

Figure 4-34

Well, not too terribly exciting, and it certainly does not look like he is fearful. The left arm is fine, because it looks as if he has caught himself after he fell. However, Figure 4-34 makes him look like he is getting ready to go to sleep or that he's eaten a big meal and needs to relax for a bit. The eyes are closed somewhat. If you were fearful or frightened of something, would your eyes be nearly or completely shut? Of course not. You *want* to see what is coming after you. Something needs to be done with this key pose. Let's open the eyes. In fact, let's get rid of the eyelids altogether so that the eyes are wide and staring. And

Figure 4-35

let's bring the right arm up, so that he can protect himself from his off-screen assailant (Fig. 4-35).

This key pose is getting there, but it still needs a bit more work. Unless the director wants something very specific, in narrative screen and stage work, the actor generally attempts to show more face to ensure that the audience can read the emotion on the face and understand the emotion. Hence, actors will sometimes "cheat" the angle of the head to ensure that the audience sees their facial action. In Figure 4-35 we cannot see the face very well, only the profile. Since we are dealing with the emotion of fear, it would behoove us to bring the face forward and move the eyes back toward the off-screen direction of the assailant. In addition, let's bring the left leg forward a bit. Remember from the last example the idea of appendages being brought into the body if we are ashamed? The same rule can apply here, only this time we are afraid that whatever is attacking us may beat our limbs, so we bring them closer to our body, except our arms, which we use to instinctively protect ourselves (Fig. 4-36).

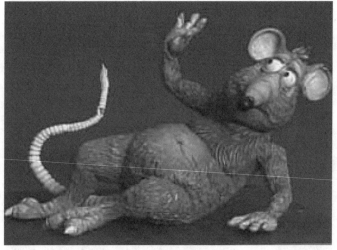

Figure 4-36

The audience now sees the fear in the rat's eyes and his reaction as he defends himself.

Now that we have a basic understanding of pose and expression, we will now explore one of the most difficult aspects of animation, the walk cycle.

CHAPTER 5

Walk and Run Cycles

Regardless of whether it is done in cel, stop-motion, or cgi, a convincing walk cycle is one of the most difficult things to accomplish in any kind of animation. A lot happens when a character walks from point A to point B:

- The body's shifting of weight from one leg to another
- The rotation of the hips
- Movement of the arms
- Torso movement
- Head movement
- Shoulder movement

Translation and Rotation

There are two primary ways a body manipulates itself when moving by itself through space:

1. Translational (sometimes called Positional) Movement
2. Rotational Movement

Since stop-motion uses a three-dimensional model that exists in three-dimensional space, this space can be broken down into three primary axes, with X moving forward and backward, Y going up and down, and Z moving side to side (Fig. 5-1).

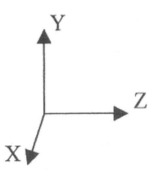

Figure 5-1

Translations deal with linear straight-ahead movement and includes a body or one of its appendages (arm or leg) moving on one or more of these axes. This movement can be:

Forward or backward (Figs. 5-2, 5-3)

Figure 5-2

Figure 5-3

Up and down (Figs. 5-4, 5-5)

Side to side (Figs. 5-6, 5-7)

Rotational movement deals with joints that work off a pivot. Such joints would include elbows, knees,

Figure 5-4

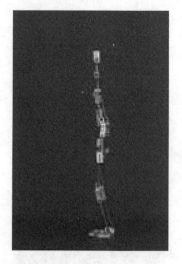

Figure 5-5

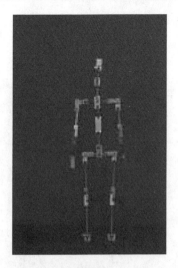

Figure 5-6

hips, neck joints, verte-brae, fingers, ankles, eye-balls, and ears. In short, any object that is at-tached to the character in some form or another that can be manipulated through rotation, as a hinge.

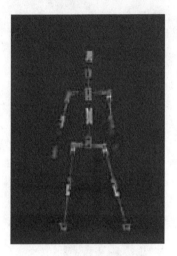

Figure 5-7

Psychology of a Walk

No two animal species walk in exactly the same way. In fact, no two humans walk in exactly the same way. A walk gives us character, and can tell others about our personality and how we are feeling at any given moment. A person who carries his head high and back arched and move straight forward is a person who might be self-confident, self-absorbed, or putting on airs. An individual who takes short, slow steps, droops his head somewhat, and walks forward with arms folded at his chest can be a person who has low self-esteem, is unsure of his surroundings, or is withdrawn and keeps to himself. And a person who walks at a leisurely pace, observing his surroundings with a smile and his hands in his pockets, may be complacent about life or easy to please.

Very few of us think about walking. Like speak-

ing, it is something we have been doing all our lives. For actors, however, it is a very good practice to con-tinually observe people and animals and their idioms in order to understand personality. Even mobile non-organic characters (such as walking machines) have some sort of personality. *The Empire Strikes Back* (1979, 20th Century–Fox) showcases the AT-AT's, gigantic quadruped walking machines that move ponderously through the snow of the ice planet Hoth. To prepare for the stop-motion animation of these mechanical be-hemoths, the animators studied the movements of ele-phants (not copying the movements exactly, but using the footage as a point of departure), imbuing the mod-els with subtle animal-like personalities and idioms.

For the 1963 Columbia Pictures fantasy film *Jason and the Argonauts*, animator Ray Harryhausen was faced with the task of bringing to life a gigantic statue made of bronze (a stop-motion puppet) to destroy Jason and his men while they are collecting food and water on a small island. Harryhausen realized that it was not enough to give the creature (hundreds of feet tall) a standard human walk. He carefully considered the following: It is made of bronze, and it is 300 feet tall or more. Since it was made of metal, it would need to walk in a slightly jerky, mechanical manner, stiff and top heavy. And because of its immense height, it would need to move somewhat slowly, in a ponderous and threatening manner. The final result, when com-posited with the tiny live-action humans and accom-panying music and sound effects, is one of fantasy filmdom's greatest and most chilling moments.

Mechanics of Joints

To reiterate, a walk encompasses both rotational and translational action. The knee, however, rotates forward or backward. The ankles rotate up and down, on their own axes, and side to side. The hips allow the legs to rotate on the legs' axes.

The shoulders are exclusively rotational and can move radially (in all directions), while the elbow ro-tates as a hinge (i.e., forward or backward), the wrist can rotate up and down and side to side, while the forearm rotates on its own axis via the radius and the ulna. The fingers are hinged.

Quadruped creatures share certain physiological amenities and yet differ when it comes to conveying the action and movement of that particular species. For example, a dog and a cat have the same basic physiological bend in their legs, but psychologically they behave quite differently. A komodo dragon and an alligator both have a tail and four legs, but they do not walk or behave the same. And while a gorilla and a human have similar physical attributes, they move quite differently. A human will not walk on all fours, but a gorilla's long arms will allow it to do so quite easily and naturally. Whether it is running along the ground or through its web, a spider (some 30,000-plus species are known) hops, skips, jumps, runs, and springs differently contingent on the species.

In short, the world is profoundly rich in diversity when it comes to personality-walking behavior, and it will behoove the actor/animator to observe and study this remarkable diversity on a regular basis. The more you know, the better equipped you will be to apply your knowledge of movement to your animated characters.

This chapter will illustrate the physiological walking and running mechanics of two-, four-, six-, and eight-legged creatures.

Key Posing and In-Betweening for Stop-Motion Animation

Remember that cel and computer animation allow one to refer to previous key paper drawings, or digital key frames in the software timeline. In stop-motion, however, only one puppet is used during the manipulation process of single-frame cinematography. The animator must therefore begin the animation process at frame 1 (the first key pose) and plow through the shot, filling in the in-betweens as he goes along, hitting the next key frame, generating more in-betweens from that, hitting the next key pose, and so on until the shot is completed. This is called **straight-ahead animation, linear animation** or **through animation**. Stop-motion animation is a linear process and does not allow the animator to

skip to a key pose and change or delete it, go back to a previous in-between and tweak that pose, go forward to another key pose and alter that pose, and so on. Since it is linear, how does one generate key poses as well as the in-betweens? Let's explore this.

THE POP-THROUGH

Remember, the most important aspects of imparting a performance in animation is to analyze the action to be generated and then generate the representative key poses that will help convey that performance successfully to the audience. Without proper keys, the action can be ambiguous and dull. The keys set the performance while the in-betweens work more toward timing as well as smoothing out the action.

To confirm that the keys will work, it is best to create a **pop-through**. This is basically a test to ensure that the audience will understand the emotion of the action. A pop-through is comprised of the key poses (sans in-betweens), and each key is held for a certain length of time, usually 15 frames or more. The actual frames held are fairly arbitrary and is dependent on how long the director wishes to have the pop-through play. Generally, a one-second hold (24 frames for film and 30 frames for video) is sufficient to play through the keys to get a feel for the performance and to see if it is working (Figs. 5-8, through 5-12).

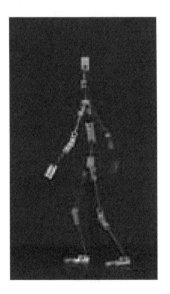
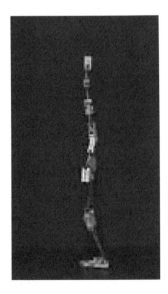

Figure 5-8   Figure 5-9

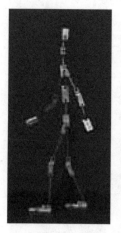

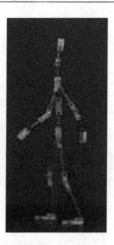

Figure 5-10   Figure 5-11   Figure 5-12

Once these poses are working, the next issue is to retain their poses during the linear animation process of stop-motion. One can commit these key poses to memory, but that can be very difficult. Here are two techniques that can help the stop-motion animator stay on track with hitting his/her key pose marks.

Tracing Lines on Clear Acetate, Hung Over a TV Screen

With the advent of video and TV monitors, stop-motion animators can now see the image of the puppet on the screen. This is very useful for the animator. The video camera is plugged into a TV monitor so that the image of the puppet is seen on the TV. By hanging a piece of clear acetate or a clear animation cel over the screen, one can take a marker and draw lines that represent the positions of the puppet.

As the puppet is moved in space, it can be lined up with the individual lines on the acetate, thereby following the planned movement of the animator. And since stop-motion is linear animation, those lines represent key poses and can be marked as such on the screen.

The Biped Walk

Bipeds include all primates and humans, though humans are exclusively biped and walk upright, while primates alternate between walking on twos and also on all fours.

Center of Gravity

Everything on the surface of the planet is affected by gravity. Resting objects can remain resting with little effort. However, once that object stands up and begins to move about, gravity plays a much greater role, and the need for that moving object to fight gravity and find its center of gravity becomes critical if it is to succeed in moving through its environment. If a moving object's center of gravity is wrong, the movement will look unnatural and fail to convince an audience that it is normal walking behavior. Figure 5-13 demonstrates a bipedal creature (human) with both feet on the ground and its center of gravity between the legs, which is correct.

In Figure 5-14, the right leg has risen to take a step forward. Notice how the body's center of gravity still remains in the center of the legs.

This is incorrect because a bipedal creature must shift its center of gravity to the leg that is still on the ground in order to keep from falling over. Figure 5-15 corrects this by placing the center of gravity over the leg that is on the ground.

A single step has a "push-off" (ascending) and a "coming to rest" (descending) action. For example,

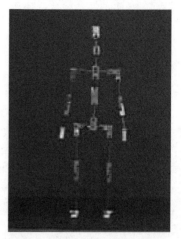

Figure 5-13

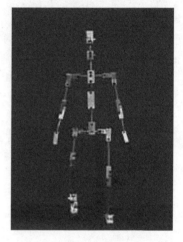

Figure 5-14

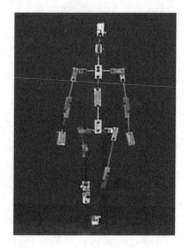

Figure 5-15

when the back leg pushes the body forward, it does not immediately lift off the ground. If it did, the person might fall backward. There are two things that occur when a body begins a walking action:

1. Pushing off the back foot begins the forward motion.
2. This movement forward is necessary to position the body's center of gravity so that a bipedal creature can balance on the foot that is on the ground, while lifting the back foot off to bring it forward.

When the person is at frame 6 (the halfway point of a 12-frame step), the body will shift over to the leg that is on the ground. This must be done, so that the body can balance itself on one leg. It generally takes at least three frames before the back foot can lift off the ground.

When the body comes to rest at frame 12, the leg hits the ground three frames earlier before the body comes to rest. The forward leg acts as a sort of "shock absorber," which stabilizes the body as it comes forward, preventing it from falling forward.

Now that we understand the basic mechanics of the key poses for a walk cycle, let's examine the creation of the key and in-between poses for stop-motion.

The Biped Walk Cycle

It was mentioned earlier that no two people walk exactly the same way. While humans walk on two legs, we have certain idiosyncrasies that set us apart from the next person. One person might move his arms back and forth with greater distance than the other, or take shorter steps. One person might put his hands in his pockets as he walks, while another might hardly move his arms at all. If one leg is shorter than the other, the person will walk with a limp.

Some people walk rather fast, but for the most part, people generally take their time walking. As previously mentioned, no two walks are exactly the same, but often the

timing of a walk cycle is fairly common. To make this concept easy to understand, we will use a standard 24-frame walk cycle (which equals one second of screen time per cycle if shooting on film). In a standard, conventional walk forward, one leg remains on the ground, and the body uses the solidity of the ground and the bottom of the back foot to push the body forward. At some point, the leg lifts off the ground.

A human must take two steps to complete one cycle in a walk. For this illustration, we will use a 24-frame cycle. Since one full cycle equals 24 frames, it stands to reason that the first step will equal 12 frames. And the second step will equal 12 frames, completing the required 24 frames for the cycle. The leg that was originally ahead of the other at the beginning of the cycle is now ahead of it again. This is why it is called a cycle. Let's examine the halfway point of the first step, six frames total (Figs. 5-16, through 5-21).

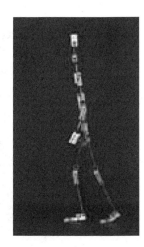

| **Figure 5-16** | **Figure 5-17** | **Figure 5-18** |

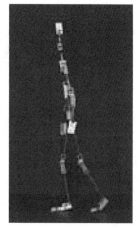

| **Figure 5-19** | **Figure 5-20** | **Figure 5-21** |

As the back leg comes up, it is still quite close to the ground. Unless the legs need to be exaggerated going up and down (such as in a dance or a clown performing in a circus), the feet remain quite close to the ground. This is why we sometimes find ourselves tripping on things that we don't notice (such as a tiny rise in a sidewalk, and sometimes even our own feet!).

And now for the last half of the first step, another six frames, thus completing the first step of the cycle (Figs. 5-22, through 5-27).

Now we do the same for the second step, thus completing the cycle (Figs. 5-28, through 5-39).

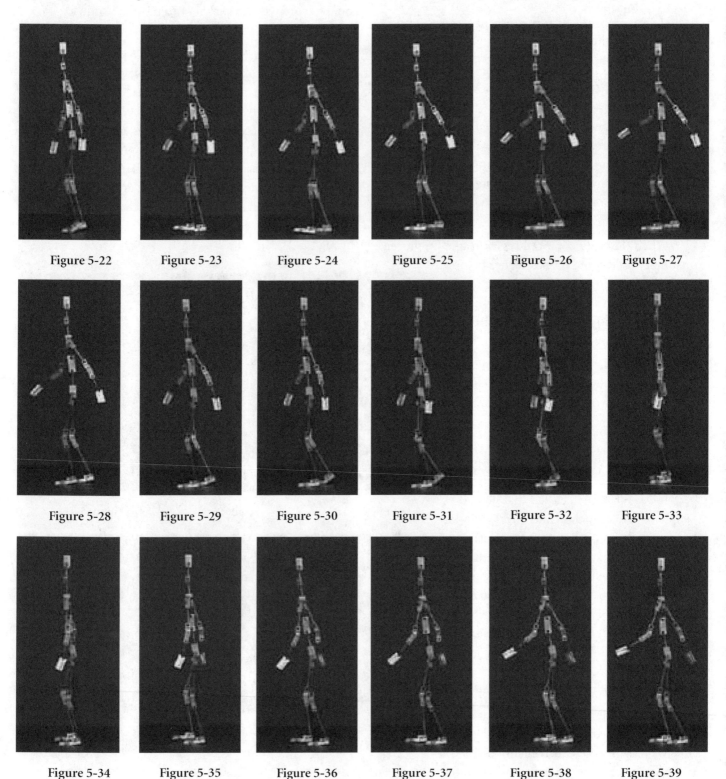

Figure 5-22   Figure 5-23   Figure 5-24   Figure 5-25   Figure 5-26   Figure 5-27

Figure 5-28   Figure 5-29   Figure 5-30   Figure 5-31   Figure 5-32   Figure 5-33

Figure 5-34   Figure 5-35   Figure 5-36   Figure 5-37   Figure 5-38   Figure 5-39

THE SNEAKY WALK

Body language says a great deal while we are walking. Posture and pose is everything in any kind of walk. A person who wants to sneak up on something is going to bring his upper body down so that he cannot be seen. Lions in the wild crouch very low and use tall grass to hide themselves prior to pouncing on unsuspecting prey. They also take long sinewy steps, with pauses between the steps. A character that sneaks is tense and

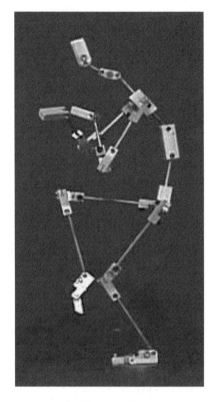

Figure 5-40

does not want to be discovered. Figure 5-40 illustrates an introductory key pose of the sneak walk.

Notice how the body is brought down with legs slightly bent. The back is hunched over to help keep the head low, and the arms are brought up to chest level, close to the body (if they are far out from the body, they may be seen). The character could take very short steps, but this does not seem to impart much of a "sneaky" feel. If, however, the character takes broad steps, with small pauses between the steps, a sense of sneaking plays out much better. Note also in Figure 5-41 how the body leans back slightly as the front leg comes up, providing the anticipation to the action.

As the body moves forward, the legs bend so that the torso is brought down low enough to make it more difficult to see (Fig. 5-42).

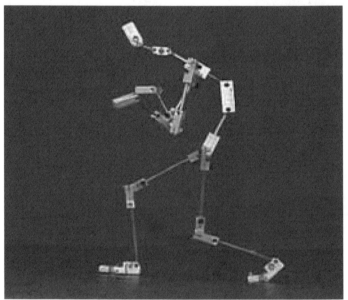

Figure 5-42

The timing of a walk such as this (mimed and without dialogue) is dependent on how motivated the sneaker wants to sneak up on the object in question and is rather subjective.

THE RUN

There are as many different numbers of run cycles as there are walk cycles. For this illustration, we will concentrate on the mechanics of a generic run.

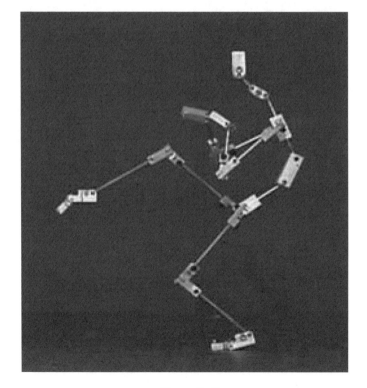

Figure 5-41

First, pose the puppet into the first key position (Fig. 5-43). Notice how the torso is curved slightly and leans into the run.

Now one must decide on the timing of the run. A 24-frame cycle may take too much time, and result in a run that appears to be slower than what is physically possible (resulting in a slow-motion run). Halving the cycle to 12 frames may be better. This means that the puppet must get his back foot to the front and on the ground by frame 6, the first half of the cycle. The legs must be wide apart. Since the first step must use six frames, these six frames would be posed as in (Figs. 5-43 through 5-48).

In this instance, frames 1, 3, and 6 are the key poses, and frames 2 and 5 are the in-betweens, filling in the action.

Frames 7 through 12 complete the 12-frame run cycle (Figs. 5-49, through 5-54).

This is a rather quick movement in which the

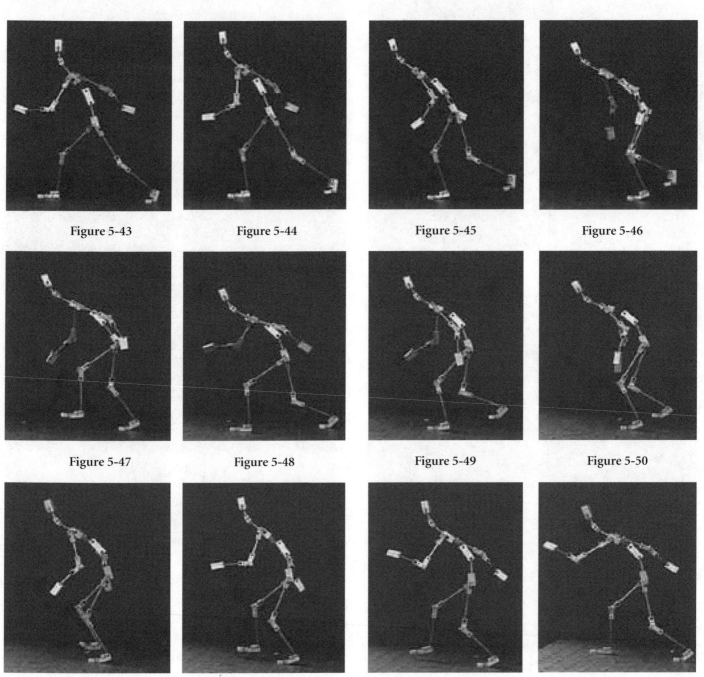

Figure 5-43   Figure 5-44   Figure 5-45   Figure 5-46

Figure 5-47   Figure 5-48   Figure 5-49   Figure 5-50

Figure 5-51   Figure 5-52   Figure 5-53   Figure 5-54

absence of blur causes considerable strobing in the animation. However, the character will nonetheless appear to be moving at a running pace and help sell the illusion that a run has indeed taken place.

When a human runs in real life, there is a "lifting-off" period in which the legs, for a brief moment, both leave the ground. In the above example, this did not happen. There are, however, a few ways this lift-off can be accomplished. One way is with the use of an aerial brace.

As its name implies, an aerial brace is a device that hangs over the animation tabletop and above the puppet, out of camera range. They can be either motion controlled or built as simply as hanging a camera tripod upside-down over the track. The following example demonstrates the latter technique (Fig. 5-55):

The rig usually consists of a series of tracks that allows the tripod to move from side to side or backward and forward over the set and puppet. Since the tripod has an up and down column in its center, a spindle of some type with turning knobs can be

bolted or c-clamped onto this column. Some tripods have a crank that allows the cameraman to raise or lower the column. Thin wires or clear, small monofilament fishing line is looped onto the knobs on the spindle, and the other ends of the wire are either looped around the puppet or the wire/thread can be inserted into the foam of the puppet via a long sewing needle and then tied. This arrangement now allows the animator to not only raise or lower the tripod column, but he/she can also turn the knobs, lengthening or shortening the wire/string. Either technique will raise or lower the puppet. The wire, string, or thread can be painted out if need be to match the color of the background (Fig. 5-56).

Another probably more economical and quick way to get both feet off the ground is with the use of washers that can be found at most hardware stores.

Figure 5-56

As the reader already knows, any stop-motion puppet is anchored to the table by drilling a hole through the table itself. A screw is then inserted through this hole from beneath the table and screwed into the tapped hole of the puppet's foot.

Look at Figure 5-57, which is divided into parts A through D. In part A, the puppet has both feet anchored to the table, though the legs are quite far apart, to suggest that a running action is taking place. In Figure B, the puppet's back leg goes forward to prepare for the leap forward as it runs. In Figure

Figure 5-55

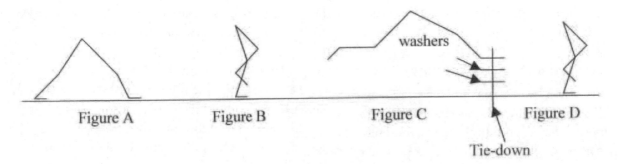

Figure A   Figure B   Figure C   Figure D

washers

Tie-down

Figure 5-57

C, the puppet has leaped into the air. Since a washer has a hole in its center, the screw can pass freely through the washers. These washers will lift the puppet off the table (C), giving the illusion that both feet have momentarily left the ground. The more washers you place beneath the foot, the higher the puppet will seem to jump. Since these washers are only on the screen for one frame, it is remote that the audience will see them. To further camouflage their appearance, the washers can be painted with the same paint that was used to paint the floor of the miniature set. The puppet finally (D) lands on one foot as the back leg goes forward.

MIMICKING EXHAUSTION

I was once teaching a stop-motion class and gave my students an assignment: Animate your puppet as if it were completely exhausted as it walks. One student (a very good animator) came in with an animation in which the puppet was sleepwalking (arms stretched out before him and walking upright). The puppet looked like it was asleep, but it didn't look physically exhausted.

The student equated being tired with being asleep. This

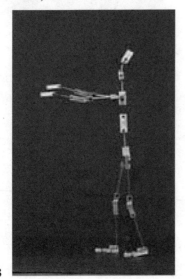

Figure 5-58

is generally true, but he then assumed that if the character was sleepwalking, then it (being asleep) must be exhausted, and if it was sleepwalking, then the audience would understand that the character is exhausted. Not so. (Fig. 5-58).

Lesson to learn from this: Make sure you have the correct interpretation of what you want to impart in your performance, or your audience will not understand. Feeling tired and looking tired can be two entirely different things. If I am sleepwalking and my arms are outstretched, I am not going to look exhausted. Being exhausted means being so tired that I cannot even hold my arms up. My arms are dead weights dangling at my sides and my knees are bent. I drag my feet as I make a feeble attempt to walk forward, when in fact I am about to collapse at any moment. *That* is being exhausted (Fig. 5-59).

The Quadruped Walk

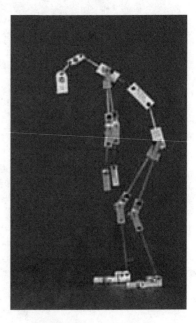

Figure 5-59

One might think of a quadruped as a human who has gotten down on all fours and walks in that fashion. An overgeneralization, of course, as the skeletal physiology of a human is quite different to that of a cat, dog, or horse.

Figure 5-60 compares the anatomical bend of a human leg to that of the back legs of a horse, dog, or cat.

While there may not seem to be significant anatomical differences between horse, cat, and dog legs, much of the character of how a particular animal walks is born out of their physiological/psycho-

Figure 5-60

logical makeup. As a horse walks forward, its head bobs very slightly forward and backward. So does a pigeon's, but it is much more acute. A dog's head does not bob nor does a cat's. A cat tends to walk forward in an extremely linear fashion and when it stops, it sits on its haunch and licks its fur or paws. A dog is a much more physical animal and will walk in a somewhat unpredictable manner, looking this way and that, demanding attention. Cats are jumping and stealth animals, while dogs are more prone to spastic playfulness. A cat's sleek, slender build enables it to crawl through tight crevices. Though horses are graz-

ing animals, their strong, slender legs are built for speed and endurance.

GENERIC QUADRUPED WALK

The mechanics of four legs working in tandem to propel a quadruped vary from species to species. Komodo dragons have a rather curious walk unlike quadruped mammals. Their front left leg lifts up at the same time as their back right leg as they move forward. As those legs come down and touch the ground, the front right leg and back left leg come up and go forward, coming to rest on the ground. However, most mammals do not walk this way. Let's explore one way they might be animated.

STAGGERING THE MOTION OF THE LEGS

The principle is that the two front legs always have one leg forward, and the two back legs have a leg forward. Two legs on one side of the body will be close together, while the two legs on the other side are far apart, as shown in Figure 61.

Since the left back leg is the leg farthest from the body, it will help push the body forward (Fig. 5-62) as the right front leg begins to lift up and go forward.

As the right front leg continues going forward, the left back leg must come up and begin moving forward (Fig. 5-63), while the right back leg and left front leg balance the body. In other words, the right front leg lifts up before the left back leg.

As the right front leg is beginning to come down to rest on the ground, the left back leg continues

Figure 5-61

Figure 5-62

Figure 5-63

Figure 5-64

Figure 5-65

Figure 5-66

moving forward (Fig. 5-64).

When the right front leg comes to rest on the ground, the left back leg is still moving forward, coming closer to the ground (Fig. 5-65).

Finally, the left back leg comes to rest on the ground, completing the first half of the cycle (Fig. 5-66).

This overlapping action helps to create a more organic feel to the movement.

HIP ROTATION

In the case of either a biped or a quadruped, it is not just enough to animate the legs and body walking forward; the body should have hip rotation as well. This rotation is very subtle during a walk, though it is a bit more prominent in a woman due to a wider pelvic area than a man's. This is much easier to see in a front or back view than a side view. Let's observe it in a front view (R.B. = right back leg; L.B. = left back leg).

The character is once again placed in its beginning walk key pose (Fig. 5-67).

As the L.B. leg lifts up, the weight is shifted over to the R.B. leg. As this shift occurs, the hips rotate slightly to the R.B. leg (Fig. 5-68).

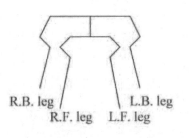

R.B. leg   L.B. leg
  R.F. leg   L.F. leg

Figure 5-67

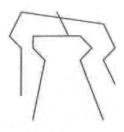

Figure 5-68

In addition, the body shifts its translation (i.e., center of gravity) to the R.B. leg as well.

The Six-Legged Walk

This group includes the ant, fly, bee, and most insects. In the case of ants, these creatures are very sporadic and random when they walk, and will hop, skip, and dart in a seemingly unpredictable manner. Like any living creature, however, they are still bound by the laws of gravity and must walk in a fashion that reflects gravity influencing their body (weight, balance, pose, and center of gravity).

Humans only have two legs, and we are constantly shifting our weight from one leg to the other in order to keep our center of balance accurate at all times while walking. In the case of the six-legged insect, there is little to no shifting required to keep its body's center of gravity stabilized, simply because there are more legs to keep everything upright.

To make the six-legged walk easier to understand, we will explore how a six-legged creature might walk using a generic move, the alternating tri-adic fashion ("tri" meaning three), and was first explained to me by animator Paul Jessel (Fig. 5-69).

This motion calls for three pairs of legs being off the ground while the other three pairs are on the ground. On the left side of the body, the two outer pairs of legs are on the ground and the middle leg is in

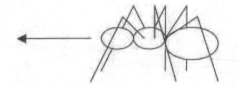

Figure 5-69

the air. While on the right side, the two outer legs are in the air, and the middle leg is on the ground. As a result, a walking "tripod" effect takes place that enables the creature to keep its balance at all times. Whenever a middle leg is on the ground, it is the only leg on that side of the body that is on the ground. Therefore, the creature may end up shifting its body toward the direction of the two outer legs that are on the ground in order to better stabilize itself. In Figure 5-70, notice how the pairs of legs behave.

Of course, this walking pattern is only a point of

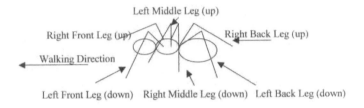

Figure 5-70

departure to what happens at the fundamental level of a six-legged walk. When the actor/animator assays the character's performance, the movement will be driven largely by the emotional content of the scene and what the character has to do (darting, jumping, spinning, scurrying, etc.). Leg movement may therefore appear sporadic and unpredictable. What *will not* change is the body's center of gravity and the need to constantly stabilize that center.

The Eight-Legged Walk

The animals in this group include the spider, the scorpion, other arachnids and their relatives as well as crustaceans. One could think of an eight-legged animal as being two quadrupeds superimposed over one another. If a six-legged creature walks by using tripod-like locomotion, it stands to reason that an eight-legged animal could walk by using a quadruped shifting of leg pairs. The spider is comprised of only two sections (rather than three like an insect):

1. The head area (cephalathorax)
2. The abdomen (back section)

The legs connect to the underside of the cephalathorax (Fig. 5-71).

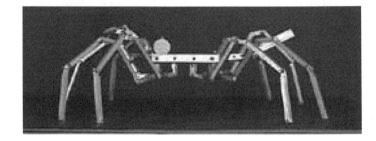

Figure 5-71

For the illustration below, only four legs on the left side are shown. The legs on the right side are doing the same thing as the left legs, mirroring the left legs' movements. The first and third pairs lift up and move forward, while the second and fourth pairs stay on the ground (Fig. 5-72).

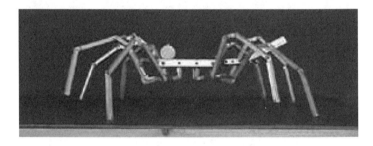

Figure 5-72

The first and third pairs come to rest on the ground (Fig. 5-73).

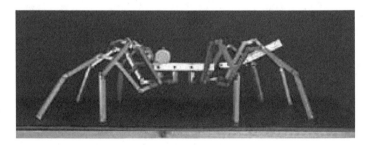

Figure 5-73

Now, the second and fourth pairs lift-off and move forward as the body is pushed ahead (Fig. 5-74).

This shifting forward of every other pairs of legs will propel the creature (Fig. 5-75).

Like any walk, however, the eight-legged walk can

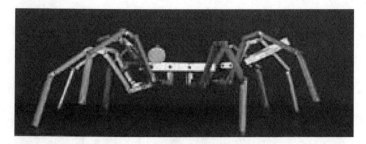

Figure 5-74

look rather mechanical if it is not given an organic feel by staggering the timing and spacing of the legs with overlapping action. The back pair of legs may come up a little later than the second pair, and so on. The im-

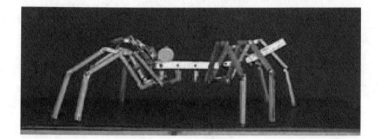

Figure 5-75

portant thing to remember is to keep the center of gravity comfortably within the body as it walks, or the movement will appear unnatural.

Using the principles of key pose that we learned earlier, let's have Mr. Rat walk through a haunted house. Let's get him into the first initial pose so that the audience feels his emotion (Fig. 5-76). The eyes are staring widely and he has drawn his tail into his body, holding it for protection and a sense of safety.

Figure 5-76

In Figure 5-77 he takes his first step, but it is a short step. He is cautious and senses that he should go slowly through the house. He begins to turn his head to look the other way.

As his foot comes down in Figure 5-78, he begins to take another step in Figure 5-79. He continues looking in the other direction (overlapping action).

As his foot comes down in Figure 5-80, he pauses for a moment, possibly unsure if he has heard something. He does hear something (as does the audience) and he quickly turns toward the camera and looks off-camera (Fig. 5-81).

Figure 5-77

He pauses for a moment, then looks toward the camera with a fast turn. At this point in the scene, pacing and timing should play a great part in helping to establish the "nervous" behavior of the rat, and the uncertainty of his situation. Holding on each key, then moving abruptly, moving again, holding and so on can help to communicate this to the audience.

He turns in the direction of movement and takes one more step in Figure 5-83 and then down again in Figure 5-84, leaning forward slightly toward the source of the sound.

Figure 5-78

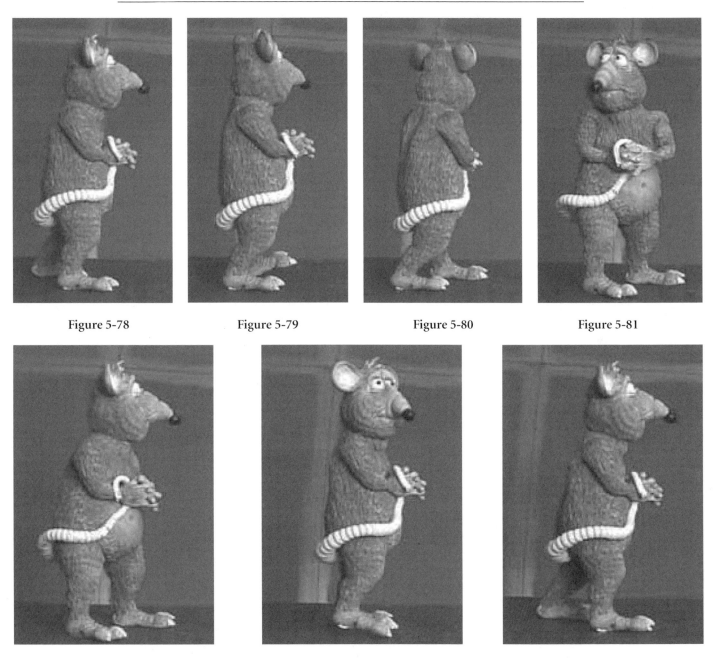

Figure 5-78   Figure 5-79   Figure 5-80   Figure 5-81

Figure 5-82   Figure 5-83   Figure 5-84

Organic motion is rarely symmetrical, even if the physiology of the creature appears to be. To reiterate, walking is one of the most difficult things to animate. The more animation you do, however, the more you will understand and apply to animation performances you will encounter throughout your career.

CHAPTER 6

Creating Replacement Figures

Replacement animation is the process of creating a series of sculptures of the same character or object. Each sculpture is slightly different from the next, and if shot in sequence, the object will appear to move. An example would be a walk cycle. The George Pal Puppetoons produced through Paramount Pictures in the 1930s and 1940s capitalized on extensive use of replacement animated figures. Replacement models do not have an internal armature (such as wire or ball and sockets).

If the director wishes an object to move 10-frame walk cycle, the sculptor would create a series of models where each model is either a key pose or an in-between (Fig. 6-1). The advantage of this process was such that the models could be used over and over again, depending on how long the character had to move, thus expediting the animation process.

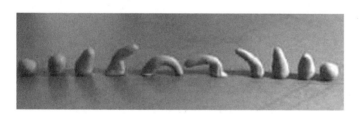

Figure 6-1

Another significant advantage of using this technique enables one to animate material that is otherwise rigid and "non-animatable," such as glass, wood, and metal. If a sculptor wishes to create a creature that is made of wood, the he/she can actually use wood to create each replacement model. And be-

cause replacement models require no armature, the illusion of seeing something made out of wood or glass moving about can be quite startling.

One common use of replacement animation is eye blinks. Note the character in Figure 6-2.

Figure 6-2

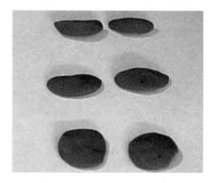

To create an eye blinking, one can use replacement eyelids made from plasticine clay or **urethane** castings (pictured are eyelids made from clay, Fig. 6-3). Since eye blinks occur rather quickly, one would only need three sets of

Figure 6-3

replacement eyelid models: eyelids slightly open, eyelids halfway closed, and eyelids fully closed.

69

The thinnest pair of eyelids would be placed on the model first because the eyelid is just beginning to close (Fig. 6-4).

Figure 6-4

A frame of film is shot. The next eyelid, which covers the eyes halfway, would be placed on the model and filmed (Fig. 6-5).

Figure 6-5

Finally, the replacement eyelids that completely covers the eyes would be placed on the model and a frame of film exposed (Fig. 6-6).

Figure 6-6

To open the eyelid, the replacements would be shot in reverse. The half-closed eyelid is placed on the model, shot, then replaced by the nearly open eyelid. When placed back at 24 frames per second, the illusion is that the model appears to quickly blink. Such attention to detail makes the character appear even more alive and natural.

Replacement Animation and Facial Manipulation for Dialogue

While there are various ways to create replacement heads, the process outlined below is an effective way to produce heads that are of uniform shape and size; the only difference is in their expressions.

Phrases are made up of words, and words are comprised of vowels and consonants. Extreme expressions of these vowels and consonants might be necessary if the dialogue track is excited and/or loud. In such cases, the model maker must know the level of emotional intensity of the dialogue.

Consider the following line:

"How many times have I told you to stop slamming the door?"

A parent who, after repeated warnings, has had enough, may say the line thus:

"HOW many TIMES have I told you to stop slamming the DOOR!!?!!!"

The parent is livid.

But this is just one interpretation. What if the parent bends down to the level of the child's face with just an inch between their noses, stares straight in the child's face, and very softly says:

"How many times have I told you (pause) to stop slamming the door?"

In this manner, the child may not immediately connect to what is said, but rather in the connection of the eyes, and what the eyes say, and it can be very disconcerting. The parent wants the child's attention, and attention he/she gets. In the mind of the child, the eyes of the parent are saying, *"I've repeatedly told you not to slam the door, and you continue to do so. Remember what I said I would do?"* Yes, the child remembers: *"Spanking."*

Vowels and consonants do not necessarily change the emotional content of what is said. The following, however, do:

- Dynamic level of the voice
- Position of the eyebrows
- How closed or open the eyelids are
- The position of the lips
- How open or closed the mouth is
- The shape of the mouth
- The lighting and composition of a shot during the performance
- Timing and pacing of the performance

A lot to consider.

Having these replacements in hand, we will now tackle the performance animation.

Creating Replacement Heads

As mentioned earlier, replacement heads can be created using many different materials. The replacements we need could be created using wood. Remember, however, that each head, while different in expression, vowel, and consonant, must still match in size from replacement to replacement. If they do not, the replacement models, during playback, will appear unstable, jerky, and inconsistent in size from frame to frame. Creating replacement heads in wood would necessitate the sculpting of each head by hand. Attempting to match the scale and size perfectly from head to head could be a rather daunting task. The challenge, then, is to create heads that match perfectly from one to the next in scale and be able to do it quickly.

A simple solution to this challenge is to create a single generic head expression, and then create an RTV-1000 mold from this original head. From this mold, many clay castings can be generated and then manipulated into the expressions, vowels, and consonants desired. Because each head would come from the same mold, they match in size perfectly. Once these heads are modified to suit the expression, more RTV molds can be made of each of these expressions, and then from these molds, urethane castings can be created and painted to be used for the final animation replacement models. Or the actor/animator can use the clay castings for animation. The disadvantage in this is if a head is accidentally dropped, the replacement head is destroyed and needs to be repaired. Urethane, being a rigid material, will withstand dropping. The advantage of clay is that it is easily pliable and can be "mushed" into any shape. Urethane cannot. Let's proceed.

There are a few ways to approach replacement faces. One is to use a generic face and then create a series of replacement mouths, which form each vowel and consonant. While this is an adequate approach, this technique does not necessarily allow for the muscles of the face (cheeks, etc.) to distort. The other approach, which we will discuss here, is to create a new head for each vowel, consonant, and extreme expression (anger, sadness, etc.).

Each head will be formed from **plasticine clay** (a common brand is Van Aken) and later reproduced in plastic urethane. Since urethane is much more durable and harder than clay, it can handle the rigors of constant replacing during the animation process. However, it would behoove us to implement a process that will enable the creation of each clay head quickly. In addition, each head must be the same size.

If they are not, the heads will change shape and size when the animation is projected back at 24 or 30 frames per second, thus destroying the illusion.

It can take too much production time to create individual heads one at a time and hope that they will match in size from head to head. To ensure that all heads are the same size and dimensions, a generic head is sculpted, and then a rubber mold is made of this head. Melted plasticine clay can then be poured into this mold to create as many heads as needed. Each of these heads can then be sculpturally altered to create a vowel or consonant, and because they come from the same mold, they will all match in shape and size.

The following materials will be needed to create these replacement heads:

1. Double boiler
2. Plasticine clay
3. Mounting boards
4. RTV-1000 mold-making material
5. Urethane casting material

To make a simple boiler, I use a wok and small pot (Fig. 6-7);

Figure 6-7

It is not recommended that plasticine clay be in direct contact with a hot surface, else the clay may scorch and burn. Plasticine clay (Fig. 6-8) has a plastic base, which is why it can be melted and poured into molds. It then solidifies as it cools. With the wok turned on, pour water into the wok and then

place the small pot inside the wok. Next, sit blocks of plasticine clay inside the pot. The heat of the hot water will then slowly melt the clay, and the clay can then be poured into a mold.

Figure 6-8

Mounting boards provide a base to sit the replacement heads onto once they have been created (Fig. 6-9).

Figure 6-9

RTV-1000 is a rubber-based mold-making material. It comes in two parts: the rubber and a curing agent (Fig. 6-10), and the rubber **vulcanizes** at room temperature when the two parts are mixed.

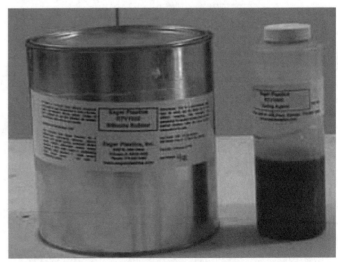

Figure 6-10

Urethane is a plastic material that comes in many kinds of hardness. Some urethanes, when they have hardened, are semi-pliable, while others set to a very hard finish and can be sanded or drilled (Fig. 6-11). Urethane comes in two parts: the activator and the resin.

Figure 6-11

To mount the heads to the boards, square brass tubing can be used (Fig. 6-12). One tube is slightly smaller than the other, so that it can slide into it. By placing the larger tube in the base of each head, the smaller tube can be glued in place on the boards. The head can then be mounted on this smaller tube protruding from the boards. In this case, we will use a ³⁄₁₆" brass square and a smaller ¹⁄₈" brass square.

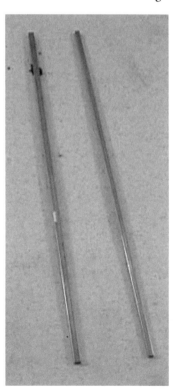

Figure 6-12

We will now create a series of replacement heads based on the vowels and consonants of the English language:

The vowels:

A – E – I – O – U (and Y, depending on the word)

The consonants:

B – C – D –
F – G – H –
J – K – L – M – N –
P – Q – R – S – T
V – W – X – Y – Z

First, let's choose something relatively simple for our replacement subject. Figures 6-13 and 6-14 offer sketches of the proposed sculpture, a clown head. We will not sculpt a hat, rather the hat can be added later after the heads are created. This will allow us to animate the hat separately once we begin animating the puppet. As the head turns this way and that and tilts up and down, the hat will flop about as secondary action.

Figure 6-13

Remember, because we will be using a series of heads of the same character, each head must match perfectly in general shape and size. To ensure this, we will create a

Figure 6-14

principal head from which all of the replacement
heads will be generated.

The post does not need to be long, just long
enough to have its end sticking from the mounting
board. Take one of the ³⁄₁₆" square rods and cut a
length of 2". Now take the ⅛" square rod and cut a
length of 3" (Fig. 6-15).

Figure 6-15

Drill a hole in one of the mounting boards
slightly smaller than the diameter of the ⅛" square
post. In this case, I used a ³⁄₁₆" drill bit (Fig. 6-16).

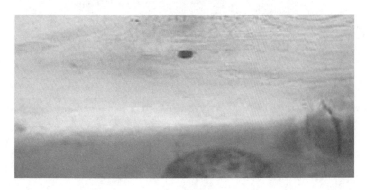

Figure 6-16

The ⅛" post will need to go into this hole. However, since the post is square and the drilled hole is
round, you will need to taper one end of the ⅛" post
on a grinder, so that the end will fit more easily into
the hole (Fig. 6-17).

Figure 6-17

Figure 6-18   **Figure 6-19**

Gently hammer the ⅛" square post into this hole
until it fits snugly (Fig. 6-18).

Now slip the ³⁄₁₆" post over the ⅛" post. To prevent the ³⁄₁₆" post from slipping all the way down the
⅛" post, you can simply use the rough edges of the interior of the post that was caused by the sawing action
of your saw blade when you cut the post off (Fig. 6-
19). You can also take a pair of needle-nose pliers and
slightly fold the edges of the end of the post into the
post opening at the top. This will keep the larger post
from slipping down the smaller one.

This will keep the ⅛"post from coming through
the top. Now that we have the larger post over the
smaller one, we can sculpt the generic clown head
over the larger post
(Fig. 6-20).

The eyes are hol-
lowed out on the sculp-
ture because later on
(when the urethane
head castings are
finished) urethane eye-
ball castings can be in-
serted into the sockets
and animated in that
fashion.

Figure 6-20

The next step is to create the mold that the urethane castings will be pulled from. An excellent mold-making material for such purposes is RTV-1000. As mentioned earlier, RTV is a flexible rubber-based compound that comes in two parts (the rubber itself and the hardening catalyst). First, we will need a container to pour the RTV into once it has been mixed. An empty, cleaned milk carton is excellent for such purposes (Fig. 6-21). Make sure you cut the carton, so that it goes higher than the sculpted head itself.

Figure 6-21

Later on when we suspend the head inside the carton, we must make sure that the head doesn't fall to the bottom when we pour the RTV into the carton. To prevent this, take two small wires and punch them through the carton (Fig. 6-22A). Wrap them around the carton and then tape over the punched holes. This will keep the RTV from flowing out through the holes when we pour it in (Fig. 6-22B).

Figure 6-22B

To successfully mix RTV, for one cup of the rubber compound, use about ⅛ cup of the blue catalyst (actually, the more catalyst you use, the quicker the mix will set). Once you have measured the two parts and poured them into the container, begin churning the mix with a wooden or plastic stick. If the mix has streaks of white in it (Fig. 6-23), it is not mixed properly.

Figure 6-23

Continue mixing until the mix has a uniform bluish color (Fig. 6-24).

Figure 6-24

Figure 6-22A

Take two strips of masking tape that will stretch across the top of the milk carton and set them aside for now (Fig. 6-25).

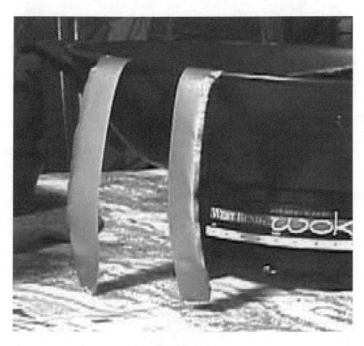

Figure 6-25

Remove the head from the post that's in the wooden support and suspend it upside down inside the milk carton, resting on the wires. Take two pieces of tape and use them to secure the post so that it sits straight up (Fig. 6-26). This will keep the post straight up and down, rather than listing to one side.

Figure 6-26

Begin pouring the mixed RTV into the carton, stopping just as the RTV comes to the base of the

head (Fig. 6-27), making sure that the bottom of the head is exposed (this will create an opening into the RTV mold, which will allow you to pour melted plasticine clay later).

Figure 6-27

It is a good idea to allow RTV to set overnight. It may appear hard after a few hours, but it may not have set at the bottom of the mold. It does not air-dry, but rather hardens chemically. "Hardens" is actually a misnomer; it sets, but it is still pliable in its texture and can be bent. Once you let go, it will snap back to its original shape.

After the RTV sets, remove the tape and pull the wires out with a pair of pliers. The carton can be cut or torn away from the RTV mold (Fig. 6-28). The mold is now exposed.

Figure 6-28

However, it is covering the clay sculpture, which will have to be exposed. To do so, take an X-Acto knife and cut around the sides of the mold (Fig. 6-29), separating the mold into two halves.

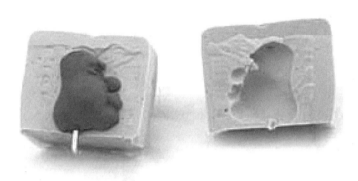

Figure 6-29

Clean out the two halves so that there is no clay in them (Fig. 6-30). Normally, a mold is sliced (or created) along the side of the object to help hide the mold seam. But because the nose is rather bulbous, it may rip off when the clay casting is removed from the RTV mold. Having the slice down the front of the face will help prevent this. The mold seam can then be cleaned up once the casting is removed.

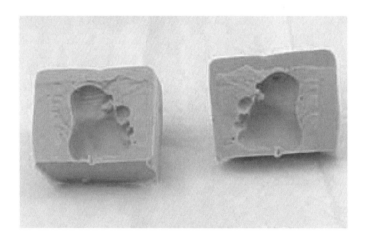

Figure 6-30

Take the two halves of the mold and put them together. This should be fairly easy, as the inconsistent cutting action of the X-Acto knife creates an uneven cut, so that the two pieces fit right together and not slide about. Now place two large rubber bands around the mold so that it is tightly shut. Turn the mold upside down. At this point, take the wok and pour water into it (Fig. 6-31).

Figure 6-31

Take some of the plasticine clay and put it inside the pot. Place the pot inside the wok (Fig. 6-32). You now have a double boiler.

Figure 6-32

Allow the water in the wok to heat until it has melted the clay (you can use a stirring stick to allow the clay to melt evenly across the pot). Line a cake pan with aluminum foil and place the RTV mold into it. Now pour the melted clay into the RTV mold (Fig. 6-33A, 6-33B). Try to pour quickly, as the clay will begin to solidify as soon as it is removed from the hot water. If it begins to clump, just put it back into the boiler again for a minute or two before resuming.

The clay should be allowed to set overnight, but you can hasten the hardening of the clay by putting

Figure 6-33A

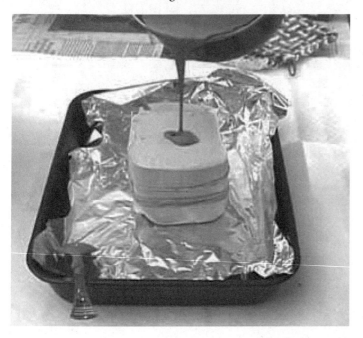

Figure 6-33B

the mold in a freezer. The point here is to make sure that the clay has sufficiently hardened before removing the mold. If the clay is still soft, you will destroy the clay casting when you try to open the mold. By putting it into a freezer or refrigerated compartment overnight, this will ensure that the clay casting is sufficiently hardened for removal (Fig. 6-34).

Occasionally, a casting coming out of a mold might have indentations, scorings, and impressions that will need to be cleaned up, such as in Figure 6-34. When this happens, simply take pieces of clay and fill in the offending areas (Fig. 6-35).

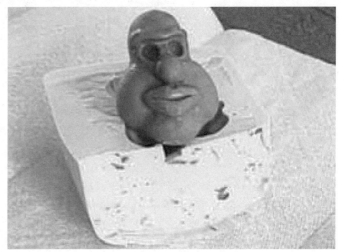

Figure 6-35

With this casting, you can now create another vowel or consonant (or extreme expression such as happy, sad, mad, etc.) by sculpting the face into the

Figure 6-36

Figure 6-34

shape desired. For this illustration, we have sculpted the clay casting into the "A" vowel (Fig. 6-36).

This replacement head can now be placed back into a refrigerated compartment to keep it from getting soft until you need it for shooting.

The rest of the alphabet can be created in this fashion, sculpting the mouth for each vowel and consonant. Once the replacements have been made, one can animate the eyebrows, moving them up or down contingent on the emotion. Eyes can be created by using either beads or by taking Sculpy clay, forming them into spheres, and painting them white. They can then be baked in an oven until they are hard. After which, they can be placed inside the sockets of the head casting. Stainless steel ball bearings work equally well for eyes.

CHAPTER 7

Reading the Dialogue Track and Creating the Exposure Sheet

Reading a dialogue track encompasses the following steps:

1. Recording the dialogue (analog or digital).
2. Placing the recording in either digital software capable of analyzing the sound or on magnetic stock and reading it through a sound synchronizer via analog.
3. Analyzing the soundtrack for its words and syllables.
4. Creating exposure sheets based on this analysis.

Before the advent of digital technology, dialogue tracks were read on magnetic stock. In the case of 16mm motion-picture film, the soundtrack was transferred to magnetic stock, which is itself 16mm wide, complete with sprocket holes. The sound reader would then run this "mag" stock over the sound heads of a synchronizer and break down the words and syllables by listening through some speakers as he/she created the exposure sheets. While this technique is still in practice, I am going to explain the digital application of reading a dialogue track here, as it is simpler and requires less expensive (and probably increasingly archaic) equipment.

An extremely user-friendly software currently on the market for reading dialogue tracks digitally is Magpie Pro, developed by Thirdwishsoftware.com. Magpie Pro allows one to open a sound file in its audio track so that the .wav can actually be seen. As the audio line is scrubbed with the left and right arrows of one's keyboard, one can hear the individual syllables and accents of each word. One can also play the sound continuously or one can slow it down to a crawl for more detailed analysis. Another advantage of using Magpie Pro is its capability of generating blank exposure sheets in preparation for laying in the syllables and words, with the dialogue track visible to the right of the frame numbers. For example, you have already loaded your dialogue file into Magpie Pro. Now, go to File–Print.

The Print window will appear. Select "Print."

After a moment (and provided that you have the software on your computer), Adobe Acrobat will launch and within it will be exposure sheets showing the sound file within its sheets. Print them out.

Let's assume that an actor has recorded the following lines from Shakespeare's *Hamlet*:

Alas, poor Yorick! I knew him, Horatio.

A man of infinite jest, of most excellent fancy.

The length of your sound file will determine the page count of your exposure sheets. In the case of our "*Alas, poor Yorick*" dialogue, this comes out to four pages (Figs. 7-1, 7-2, 7-3, 7-4).

In an actual animation production environment, a dialogue reader would listen to the reading/recording of the actor. This performance interpretation will

81

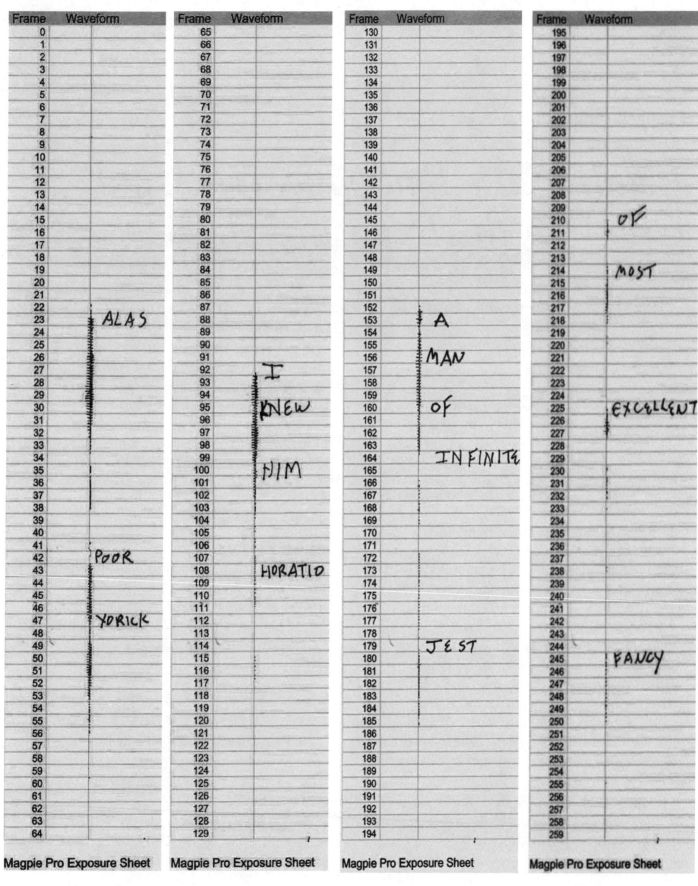

Figure 7-1   Figure 7-2   Figure 7-3   Figure 7-4

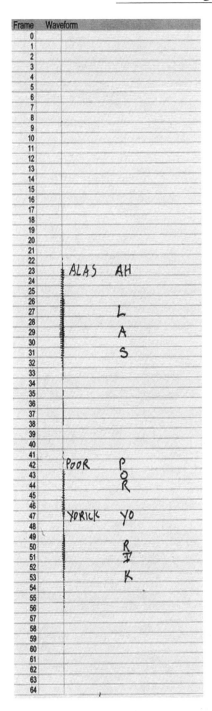

Figure 7-5

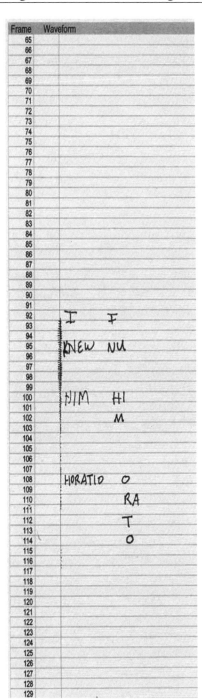

Figure 7-6

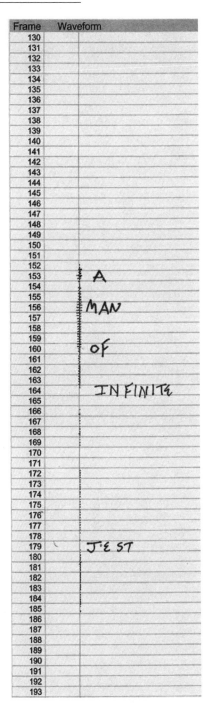

Figure 7-5

help determine how the animator would approach creating the replacement heads as well as the performance of the puppet itself. In the reading of the track, the animator discovers that it takes 259 frames to voice this line (or a little over eight seconds at 30 frames per second).

First, analyze one word at a time. The point here is to find the beginning of each word at its proper frame. The beginning of the word "*Alas*" starts at Frame 23.

The word "*Poor*" begins at Frame 43, and so on. As long as the beginning of each word's frame is correct, the timing will be hit once the lip sync is played back.

Once the beginning of each word is found and recorded on the exposure sheet, the next step is to begin breaking down those words into their syllabic components and recording those syllables at their appropriate frames on the exposure sheets. Figures 7-5, 7-6, 7-7, and 7-8 provide these syllabic breakdowns.

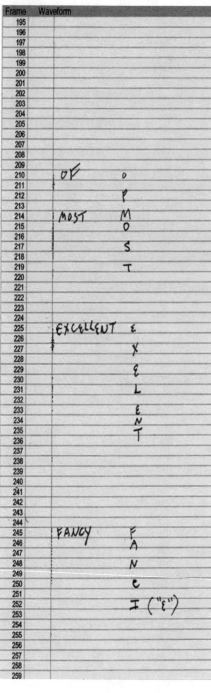

Figure 7-8

We are now faced with a curious convention (Fig. 7-9). If we take a look at the first word, "*Alas,*" we discover that it can be broken down into two syllables. "A–las." However, the actual mouthing of the word requires that we use four different positions of the mouth, and could be broken down thus: "A–l–a–s." Try mouthing this word yourself, going slowly, so that you can feel the different positions. Say it in front of a mirror, so that you can actually see the positions. In addition, there can be two different ways to position the mouth to say the "*A*" syllable: "*Aye*" (such as in the word *Apricot*) or "*Ah*" (as in the

word *Append*). In the "*Aye*" sound, the mouth is stretched horizontally, while in the "*Ah*" sound the mouth is stretched vertically. The word "*Alas*" uses the "*Ah*" sound, and therefore would require a replacement head wherein the mouth is formed vertically. Figure 7-9 illustrates the four mouth positions required to voice "*Alas.*" Phonetically, it breaks down in this fashion: "*Ah–L–A–S.*" "*Ah*" (as in *Append*)–"*L*" (with the tongue showing slightly between the lips)–"*A*" (as in the word ("*At*")—"*S*" (with the lips pursed slightly together, with the teeth together slightly and showing through the lips). In the exposure sheets, "*Ah*" begins at Frame 23 and lasts through Frame 26. "*L*" goes from Frame 27 through Frame 28. "*A*" from Frame 29 through 30, and "*S*" from Frame 31 through 32 (the actual decay of the word can be seen in the .wav image that was copied into the sheets).

The word "*poor*" begins at Frame 42 but lasts only for one frame. Its "*o*" syllable begins at Frame 43, and "*r*" begins at Frame 44. When we come to "*Yorick,*" we discover that "*Y*" actually sounds and looks like "*o,*" and as such, the "*o*" replacement face could be used for "*Y.*" Indeed, most words beginning with "*Y*" are followed by a vowel ("Yak," "Young," "Yep," "Yippie," Yuppie"). The beginning of each of these words more or less begins on the vowel. In other words, one would not necessarily need to create a replacement face for "*Y,*" because the vowel of a Y word is sounded first. Therefore, just begin the word with the vowel in question (Fig. 7-10).

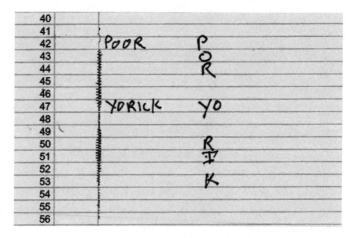

Figure 7-10

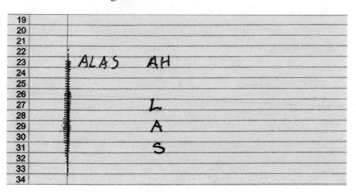

Figure 7-9

The next three words, "*I knew him,*" run quite close together. "*I,*" at Frame 92, only needs the "I" sound ("eye") and lasts through Frame 94. At Frame 95, the word "*new*" is pronounced "*nu,*" but in voicing the "*N*" consonant, the lips are brought close together, and then the vowel comes later. Therefore, "*new*" would need two replacement faces. At Frame 100 through 102, "*him*" is spoken. Since "*H*" is usually followed by a vowel in the English language, there is little to no need for an "*H*" replacement face because (like the "Y") the vowel is heard first (Fig. 7-11).

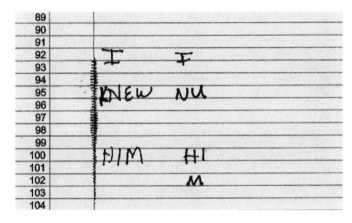

Figure 7-11

Frame 108 introduces us to "*Horatio,*" and the word lasts through Frame 114. Once again, since this word begins with an "*H,*" we will only need the "*o*" replacement face. At Frame 110, we see the "*ra*" sound. This will require two replacements: one in which the mouth is configured into the "*r*" (lips close together and pushed out very slightly) and the replacement "*a*" (as in the word "*aye*"). The "*T*" at Frame 112 through 113 would need to have a re-placement face reflecting the shape "*tee,*" and if one is to pronounce it, one would discover that one only needs to use the "*e*" replacement face. Finally, at Frame 114, one would use "*o*" (Fig. 7-12).

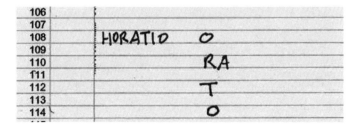

Figure 7-12

The "*A*" at Frame 153 would need a replacement face reflecting the shape used for pronouncing "*Aye.*" "*Man*" at Frame 156 requires three shapes: one with the mouth closed (for "*m*"), the second for "*A*" (the shape of which suggesting "*at*"), and the third shape as "*n.*" The word "*of*" is broken down into two shapes: "*o*" *and* "*f,*" in which the shape requires that the upper teeth be placed slightly over the lower lip (Fig. 7-13).

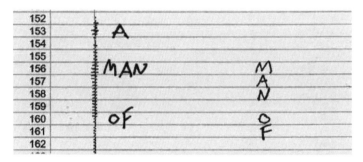

Figure 7-13

"*Infinite*" (Fig. 7-14), at Frames 164 through 172, is a bit of a challenge, in part because during the recording the actor said this word very quickly. As such, all of the syllables have flowed together, with each one lasting barely one frame. In analyzing the word, it could conceivably be broken down to follow these replacement shapes:

"*Eh–n — f–ih — n — eh — t*"

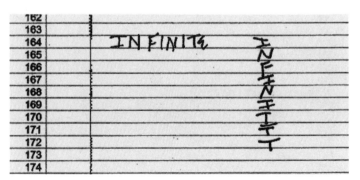

Figure 7-14

The "*f*" is especially needed because the mouth is closed whenever this consonant is voiced. This is because closing and opening the mouth and lips helps us to register the separation of words as we ob-serve speech.

"*Jest*" in Figure 7–15 lasts for seven frames. "*J*" requires a replacement shape in which the lips stick out slightly with the teeth not quite touching (similar to "*r*"). "*Eh*" should be used for the "*e,*" and the word can be finished using "*esss.*" The "*s*" sound demands that the teeth be together and slightly slowing through the lips. Since the "*t*" requires that the teeth be together as well, "*jest,*" the word, can be finished off with the "*s*" replacement face.

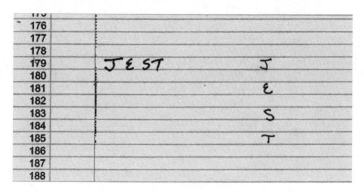

Figure 7-15

The next two words are relatively simple: "*of*" and "*most.*" Frames 210 through 213 require "*o*" and the upper-teeth-on-the lower lip "*f.*" Each lasts two frames. "*Most*" can use a closed neutral mouth ("*m*"), then leading into "*o.*" And, like the word "*jest,*" "*most*" can be finished using only the "*s*" replacement head, dispensing with "*t.*"

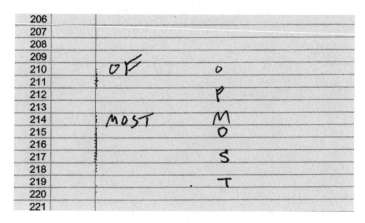

Figure 7-16

The word "*excellent*" (Fig. 7-17) could be broken down into the following shapes:

"*eh — s — eh — l — eh — n — t*"

"*eh*"— Frames 225–226

"*s*"— Frames 227–228 ("*x*" and "*z*" are very similar to "*s*" in mouth shape)

"*eh*"— Frames 229–230

"*l*"— Frames 231–232

"*eh*"— Frame 233

"*n*"— Frame 234

"*t*"— Frame 235

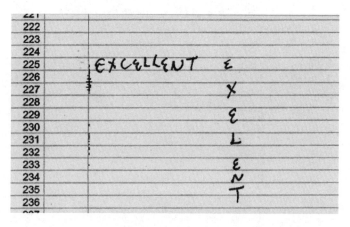

Figure 7-17

The concluding word "*fancy*" would be broken down thus:

"*f*"— Frame 245

"*ah*"— Frames 246–247

"*n*"— Frames 248–249

"*e*"— Frame 252 (as in the word "*even*")

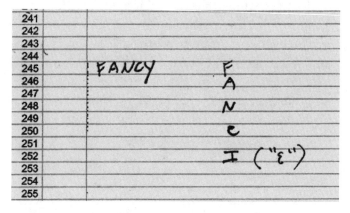

Figure 7-18

Having gone through this chapter, the reader must now be aware that not every letter in the English alphabet is pronounced precisely the same from one word to the next. The "*e*" used in "*even*" is not mouthed exactly the same way as the "*e*" in the word "*ever.*" Any word beginning with an "x," as in xylophone, is actually pronounced "z," but "z" is very much like "s" in the formation of the mouth, and so on. The only real way to succeed at proper lip sync is to pay careful attention to how words must be formed using the mouth, teeth, and tongue, and to inject these visual forms into your replacement sculptures. If you are astute at observing these relationships and have correctly read your exposure sheets, your lip sync will succeed.

Concluding Remarks

Technology changes. However, it is difficult to change with the times when one is comfortable with the tools one has learned over the years from one's craft. A person who was weaned on stop-motion animation may not readily embrace computer animation technology. Likewise, an individual who has learned the photochemical process of motion-picture shooting may not immediately fall in love with digital technology.

Regardless of the technology used, filmmaking is the art of telling a story through the use of a plot and performance. Photochemical and digital technology are only tools to further the aim of the storyteller and are by-products of the process, not a means to an end. The success of a film rests in the creative spark and talent of those creating the art. Audiences will not fall in love with your Sony digital camera or 35mm Panavison camera, but they can fall in love and connect with your characters. Human nature remains relatively constant through the ages. We desire love, friendship, a family, a beautiful sunset, our favorite music, and a great story. We are, by and large, intensely romantic and social creatures (whether we admit it or not), always striving to better ourselves and those around us.

This book and its companion volumes, (*Stop-Motion Armature Machining* and *Stop-Motion Puppet Sculpting*) are only by-product information leading toward a higher goal: to create, through the medium of animation, art that can help explain the human condition (good and bad) to the world.

As you go on in your endeavors as a filmmaker and animator, may I wish you the very best in furthering and embracing the art form in ways that are personal, fulfilling, inspired and inspiring to a world that never ceases to crave a reflection of itself in all that is hopeful, noble, loving and grand in life. This is, after all, the aim of any great art.

Tom Brierton
December 2005

Glossary

Absorbed — light that has been absorbed by a surface and does not bounce back to the eye.

Ambient light — light that is lacking shadow, such as on an overcast day when clouds block the sun's light.

Anticipation — in animation, the process of setting up an action. If a character must kick a ball with his foot, he will first bring his leg back before kicking the ball. The audience "anticipates" that the character will kick the ball.

Aperture — the film plane of a camera, i.e., the opening of the camera that the film travels across during exposure.

Arc — in animation, an imaginary line that an object travels along during a given move.

ASA/ISO — a rating system for motion-picture film.

Atmospheric perspective — as objects recede farther into the distance (such as a mountain range), they become less distinct visually and lose their hue, moving more to the lighter side.

Barn door — in lighting, a series of hinged panels that connect to an overhanging light, such as a spotlight. Moving these panels on their hinges allow the cinematographer to redirect a beam of light in a wide or narrow angle.

Blocking — the process in which a director plans out the principle action, movement, and/or placement of characters within a scene for a film or stage play.

Camera nodal — the center of a camera lens and/or the act of moving the camera in such a way that it can pan, tilt, pitch, and yaw at its nodal point.

Charge Coupled Device (C.C.D.) — a digital technology that allows a camera to record color through electronic means.

Catalyst — in storytelling, a device that aids in a character's emotional, mental, spiritual and/or physical change.

Color temperature — the measurement of an object's heat intensity as it burns.

Conflict — a device in storytelling that causes a character or characters to be emotionally, physically, and/or mentally challenged in his/their situation.

Content — the subject matter of a story, painting, musical composition, architecture, and so forth.

Contact printed — a photochemical process in which one piece of film is placed in contact with another to create another image.

Depth of field — the range of acceptable sharpness of a lens, when the lens is focused at infinity. The smaller the f-stop opening (of a lens), the greater the depth of field of that lens.

Ease-in — in animation, the process of allowing an object to gradually slow down.

Ease-out — in animation, the process of allowing an object to gradually accelerate.

Electromagnetic spectrum — a wide range of electromagnetic energy in the known universe (such as gamma and ultraviolet rays, as well as visible light).

Fill light—A light on a set that softens the shadows of the key light source.

Filter—a flexible or hard piece of semitransparent colored material that goes over the camera lens to change the color of light.

Fixed focal-length lens—sometimes referred to as a prime lens, a lens that is set to only one distance (i.e., 12mm, 18mm, 25mm, 50mm, etc.) and cannot be lengthened or shortened on its own, as opposed to a telephoto lens, which can.

Follow-through—in animation, the continuation of a motion after the main motion of an object has been performed. The action continues through the arc or curve, "following-through" to its completion. An example would be a baseball pitcher; the pitcher winds up to throw (anticipation), he throws the ball (action), and his arm swings round his body to complete the motion (follow-through).

Forced perspective—placing one object closer to the camera while other objects are placed farther away in the same scene. For example, during location photography, a detailed miniature castle three-feet high is placed close to the camera and framed to look as if it is sitting on a faraway hill in the landscape, while actors portraying knights are placed at the bottom of the hill. The illusion is that the castle appears to be an actual castle rather than a miniature. The advantage of this technique is that the miniature is photographed at the same location as the actors, using the same light source (in this case, the sun). Since the trick is accomplished in the camera during the actual shooting of the actors, no process photography is needed and the visual effect is captured on the same negative.

Form and content—as it applies to fine art; form deals with the structure of a work of art, while content refers to the actual subject material of that work of art. To illustrate, a narrative play generally uses a two- or three-act structure (its form), while its material deals with the story of five nurses as they work in war-torn Europe during World War II (its content).

F-stop—a system of measuring the amount of light entering an aperture of a camera.

Gel—similar to a filter, a gel is usually placed over a light source.

HDTV—an acronym for High Definition Television.

Hold—in animation, the process of pausing action to allow the character to reflect for a moment. The action does not stop completely, but follows-through slightly to keep the action going.

Hue—the actual color of an object, in its purest form (i.e., red, green, blue, yellow, etc.).

In-between—the poses of an animated character that fill in between the key poses.

Incident light meter—a handheld device that measures the amount of light bouncing toward the camera lens from the object being photographed.

Infinite light—a light source that bathes the entire set or landscape (such as the sun).

Key light—the light on a set that illuminates the entire set. However, one can have more than one key light as well as more than one fill.

Key pose—in animation, the fundamental building block of the performance. A key pose provides the thought of what is in the mind of the character, and by itself, can tell a story.

Lens—a light-gathering device made of ground glass that fits at the front of a camera.

Metaphor—a storytelling device that compares one thing with another that is seemingly unrelated (such as the Shakespearian phrase, "All the world's a stage, and all the men and women merely players," or, "That cop hid from me with his radar, just like a spider waiting for its prey."

Mise-en-scène—in theater, the composition of the stage frame (or proscenium), the director's process of arranging the elements on the stage to create (either symbolically or literally) a certain feeling, thought, symbol, or emotion.

Montage—in film work, the cutting from one shot to another to create a thought or idea. These two shots can be related (Example 1) or they need not be (Example 2). Example 1: In shot one, two lovers embrace. In shot two, the camera is closer to them as they kiss. Example 2: In shot one, an aborigine tribesman throws a spear. In shot two, a soccer goalie jumps up to block a kicked ball. These two shots cut together suggest the goalie is going to catch the spear, though they were filmed on two separate continents.

Motion control— a process whereby a camera that as been externally motorized on a movable platform, allows for exact repeatability, which is necessary when shooting separate elements to be later combined as one image.

Motion parallax— as one travels down a highway in a car, objects nearest the car (such as trees and telephone poles) appear to move by quickly, while objects farther away (such as distant mountains, hills, or trees) appear to be hardly moving).

Narrative— a form of storytelling in which the story follows a straightforward reflection of what seems to occur in real life.

Opaque— an object that does not allow light to enter it (as opposed to a glass box).

Overlapping action— in animation, movement that is staggered during performance in an attempt to keep the performance from appearing symmetrical. For example, as the right arm lifts up to scratch the nose, the head turns to look off-screen, while the other arm gets stuck in a pocket, and so on.

Persistence of vision— the brain's ability to see an image, then hold and retain this image while another image prepares to take its place. Persistence of vision is the process that allows us to perceive a series of still images such as a motion picture as one continuous motion when projected at 24-frames per second.

Plot— the central story or idea of a novel, stage or screenplay.

Point light— a light source that emanates from a central source, bathing the surrounding area near it, such as the flame of a candle.

Pop-through— a process in stop-motion animation in which the animator films only the key poses of an action without in-between poses in an attempt to test the viability of the performance. Each key pose is held for a predetermined number of frames.

Pressure plate— a device within the intermit-tent movement of a motion-picture camera that holds and presses the film next to the aperture to prevent it from weaving during exposure.

Prime lens see **Fixed focal-length lens**

Proscenium— the frame of a theatrical stage in which the audience sees the performance.

Pull-down claw— a device within the intermittent movement of a motion picture camera that engages in the sprocket holes of movie film, pulling it down once a frame of film has been exposed.

R&D— Research and Development

Reflected— bounced off an object's surface (said of light)

Refracted— the bending of a light ray as it enters an object.

Registration pins— a device within the intermittent movement of a motion-picture camera that engages into the sprocket holes of a movie frame while it is being exposed.

Release print— a positive image print that is struck from an internegative, for distribution and exhibition in a movie theater.

Replacement animation— in stop-motion, the art of creating a series of sculptures of a character (such as a walk cycle). As each pose is photographed, it is replaced by the next sculpture and so on. When projected back, the character appears to be one character that is moving.

Resolution— the ability of film and digital technology to record sharpness and clarity of an image.

Rim light— a light source that creates a rim of light along the edge of an object.

Saturation— the amount of white mixed within a hue.

Scattering— when light shines through dense fog, its rays are scattered randomly and forms the cone angle of the light in question (such as a street lamp or car headlight).

Shutter— a device within the intermittent movement of a camera that allows or prevents light from striking a film negative.

Spacing— the distance from one pose to another of an animated character.

Spatial parallax— as a person walks forward, objects closest to him/her will appear to go by faster that objects that are farther away from them.

Specular— the amount of light that is reflected from the surface of an object.

Spotlight— a type of stage light that has a series of metal flaps (barn doors), enabling the cinematographer to position them to concentrate the beam of light to a specific area of the set.

Spot meter— a meter that can measure in a small bandwidth the light striking the surface of an area of a subject.

Squash and stretch— in cel animation, the process of allowing a character to deform by squashing down and stretching up during its performance.

Stereoscopic— the process of being able to see in three dimensions (height, width, and depth).

Surface gauge— a measuring device used primarily in the industrial trades, it has been used by stop-motion animators for decades to measure the distance of a puppet's in-between poses.

Technicolor— a photographic process developed by the Technicolor Labs in the 1930s by Herbert Kalmus and his associates, in which a special prism of the Technicolor camera split the primary colors (red, green, and blue) and recorded them onto their own negatives. These negatives were then combined to create one final film emulsion that created a full-color visual image.

Timing— the process of deciding how long or short a particular action is to take place.

Trajectory— an imaginary line in which an object travels (such as an arrow leaving a bow).

Translucent— a semitransparent surface that can appear foggy or frosted.

Transmitted— once a ray of light is refracted inside an object, it leaves the object at the same angle as it entered, and is said to be transmitted.

Transparent— Said of a surface that allows light to enter it and be reflected within its surface (such as a glass box).

Traveling matte— a special photographic process in which a foreground object (actor, etc.) is placed in front of a specially colored screen (blue, green, or yellow). By shooting the scene with special film emulsions, a number of mattes can be generated that enable one to place the foreground object over a background image that has been shot separately, thus creating a single composite of two or more images. As an actor moves across the colored screen, he/she creates their own mattte, allowing the actor to "travel" across the background.

Urethane— a material, usually in two parts (a resin and an activator), that is poured into a rubber mold. Urethane hardens through a chemical reaction, and the hardness can be anywhere from a rigid, tough shell to a softer, pliable hardness. This material is ideally suited to creating eyeballs, fingernails, teeth, eyelids, crusty surfaces such as insect carapaces, and horns.

Vulcanization— a chemical reaction that occurs when one material (such as rubber or resin) is mixed with another material (a resin or catalyst) to solidify the first material.

References

Lighting

Bergery, Benjamin. *Reflections: Twenty-One Cinematographers at Work.* Hollywood, CA: ASC, 2002.

Camera Function and Use

The American Cinematographer Manual, 8th ed. Hollywood, CA: ASC, 2001.

Lipton, Lenny. *Independent Filmmaking.* San Francisco: Straight Arrow, 1972.

Story and Production Development

Froug, William. *Screenwriting Tricks of the Trade.* Los Angeles: Silman-James, 1992.

_____. *Zen and the Art of Screenwriting: Insights and Interviews.* Los Angeles: Silman-James, 1996.

Gallagher, John Andrew. *Film Directors on Directing.* Westport, CT: Praeger, 1989.

Winder, Catherine, and Zahra Dowlatabadi. *Producing Animation.* Woburn, MA: Focal, 2001.

Performance Principles

Blair, Preston. *How to Draw Cartoon Animation.* Tustin, CA: Walter Foster, 1989.

Culhane, Shamus. *Animation from Script to Screen.* New York: St. Martin's, 1988.

Hagen, Uta. *Respect for Acting.* New York: Hungry Minds, 1973.

Hooks, Ed. *Acting for Animators.* Portsmouth, NH: Heinemann, 2000.

Redgrave, Michael. *The Actor's Ways and Means.* New York: Routledge, 1953.

Williams, Richard. *The Animator's Survival Kit.* London: Faber & Faber, 2001.

Websites of Interest

The Mole Richardson Company: http://www.mole.com/aboutus/history

Third Wish Software & Animation: http://www.third wishsoftare.com (lip synchronization software)

Index